What Readers Said About
tmux 2: Productive Mouse-Free Development

A must-have book for anyone that uses the command line daily. This is a book I have been recommending since it was first published, and I will definitely recommend it again!

➤ **Jeff Holland**
  Senior software engineer, Ackmann & Dickenson

The tricks mentioned in this book completely changed my workflow. I recommend this book to anyone who is looking to improve their workflow on the command line.

➤ **Jacob Chae**
  Software engineer, Assurant

The author always has something amazing in store for you: custom commands to fire up your development environment, customizing it, pair programming, and many use cases. This book makes you step up your game in becoming a more efficient developer.

➤ **Peter Perlepes**
  Software engineer, adaplo

I had zero tmux experience before picking up the book, and I could use tmux in my day-to-day routine after reading the book.

➤ **Nick McGinness**
  Software engineer, Direct Supply

tmux 3

Productive Mouse-Free Development

Brian P. Hogan

The Pragmatic Bookshelf

Dallas, Texas

See our complete catalog of hands-on, practical,
and Pragmatic content for software developers:
https://pragprog.com

Sales, volume licensing, and support:
support@pragprog.com

Derivative works, AI training and testing,
international translations, and other rights:
rights@pragprog.com

The team that produced this book includes:

Publisher:	Dave Thomas
COO:	Janet Furlow
Executive Editor:	Susannah Davidson
Development Editor:	Tammy Coron
Copy Editor:	Karen Galle
Indexing:	Potomac Indexing, LLC
Layout:	Gilson Graphics

ISBN-13: 979-8-88865-131-5
Book version: P1.0—February 2025

Contents

Acknowledgments

Thank you for reading this book. It's my sincere hope that this book will help you get better at what you do by making you faster and more productive.

Thank you, Chris Johnson, for initially showing me what tmux was all about and for pointing me in the right direction with my initial questions. It completely changed how I work, and it's what motivated me to share this amazing tool with everyone. It's indispensable and I'm excited to share this third edition with the world.

Thank you, Dave Thomas, for convincing me to publish the first edition of this book, and to Susannah Davidson for editing the first and second editions. I've had so many people tell me how much they learned from those editions. This edition sits on a solid foundation.

Thank you, Tammy Coron, for editing this edition. There were more changes than I anticipated, and it took far longer than we both hoped. It's been rough, but I'm grateful to you for nudging me along all those times things got slow.

Thank you, Tim Chase, Ricardo Gerardi, and Manoj Reddy for your incredibly thorough review. You found some serious show-stoppers. This book is a lot more clear, thanks to your feedback.

Thank you, Mason Egger, Alex Garnett, Michael Guerin, Ian Hogan, Jeff Holland, Jeanelle Horcacitas, Nick LaMuro, Will Langford, Amelia Mango, Brian MacDonald, Haley Mills, Sam Nelson, Caitlin Postal, Dave Rankin, Tim Simmons, Myles Steinhauser, Jessica Stodola, Adam Stodola, Lisa Tagliaferri, Erich Tesky, Candace van Oostrum, Natalia Vargas-Caba, Mitchell Volk, Chris Warren, and Mike Weber, for your continued support.

Thank you, Ana and Lisa, for your love and inspiration.

Finally, thank you, Carissa, for your love and support. Thank you for all you do for our family.

Preface

Your mouse is slowing you down.

When it was first introduced, the mouse created a new way for people to interact with computers. You can click, double-click, and even triple-click to open documents, switch windows, and select text. And thanks to trackpads, you can even swipe and use gestures to interact with your applications. The mouse, along with graphical interfaces, made computers just a little easier for the average person to use. But, there's a downside to the mouse, especially for programmers.

As you build software, you work with multiple programs throughout the course of your day. If you're a full-stack developer, you might have a database console, a local web server, and a text editor running at the same time. And you'll surely have to run your test suite and other commands. Switching between terminal windows or tabs with the mouse can slow you down. It may not seem like much, but moving your hand off of the keyboard's home row, placing it on the mouse, locating the pointer, and performing the task can eat up time and break your focus. It can also induce strain on your wrist, arm, or shoulder. That repetitive movement can cause some serious discomfort if you're not careful about how you hold that mouse.

Using tmux, you can create an environment like this right in a single terminal window, managed entirely without a mouse:

Using tmux's windows, you can easily manage a text editor and a database console, and run local web servers and tests within a single environment. You can split tmux windows into sections, so multiple apps can run side-by-side. This means you can run a text-based browser, a text-based chat client, or your automated tests in the same window as your main editor.

Best of all, you can quickly move between these windows and panes using only the keyboard. Over time, the keystrokes you use to manage your environment will become second nature to you, which will greatly increase both your concentration and your productivity.

In this book, you'll configure, use, and customize tmux. You'll manage multiple programs simultaneously, write scripts to create custom environments, and use tmux to work remotely with others. With tmux, you can create a work environment that keeps almost everything you need at your fingertips.

What Is tmux?

tmux is a *terminal multiplexer*. It lets you use a single environment to launch multiple terminals, or windows, each running its own process or program. For example, you can launch tmux and load up the Vim text editor. You can then create a new window, load up a database console, and switch back and forth between these programs, all within a single session.

If you use a modern operating system and a terminal that has tabs, this doesn't sound like anything new. But running multiple programs simultaneously is only one of tmux's features. You can divide your terminal windows into horizontal or vertical panes, which means you can run two or more programs on the same screen side by side. You can ensure these new windows or panes always open in the directory you want. You can move them from window to window and change their layout. And you can do it all without using the mouse.

You can also *detach* from a session, meaning you can leave your environment running in the background. If you've used GNU-Screen before, you're familiar with this feature. In many ways, tmux is like GNU-Screen with a lot of extra features and a more approachable configuration system. Since tmux uses a client-server model, you can control windows and panes from a central location or even jump between multiple sessions from a single terminal window. This client-server model also lets you create scripts and interact with tmux from other windows or applications.

Over the course of this book, you'll use all of these features and more.

Who Should Read This Book

Whether you're a system administrator or a software developer who spends a good part of your time using the terminal and command-line tools, this book aims to help you work faster.

If you're a software developer, you'll use tmux to build a development environment that can make working with multiple terminal sessions a breeze. And if you're already comfortable using Vim or Emacs, you'll see how tmux can accelerate your workflow even more.

If you're a system administrator or a developer who spends time working with remote servers, you'll be interested in how you can leverage tmux to create a persistent dashboard for managing or monitoring servers.

What's in This Book

This book will help you incorporate tmux into your work by taking you through its basic features and showing you how you can apply them to everyday situations.

In Chapter 1, Learning the Basics, on page 1, you'll use tmux's basic features. You'll create sessions, panes, and windows and get comfortable with basic navigation.

In Chapter 2, Configuring tmux, on page 15, you'll redefine many of the default keybindings and customize how tmux looks as you build your own configuration file from scratch.

In Chapter 3, Scripting Customized tmux Environments, on page 41, you'll script a custom development environment using the command-line interface, configuration files, and the tmuxinator program.

After that, you'll work with text in Chapter 4, Working With Text and Buffers, on page 53. You'll use the keyboard to move backward through the buffer, select and copy text, and work with multiple paste buffers. You'll also integrate tmux with your system clipboard.

Next, in Chapter 5, Pair Programming with tmux, on page 63, you'll set up tmux so that you and a coworker can work together on the same codebase from different computers.

Finally, Chapter 6, Workflows, on page 73 introduces more advanced ways to make you more productive. You'll manage windows, panes, and sessions; create popup windows; build custom menus; and explore tmux plugins.

Changes in the Third Edition

This new edition has some notable changes from the second edition. tmux 3 introduced several backward-incompatible changes to tmux's configuration syntax that this edition addresses. It also introduced some new features. Here's what's changed in the third edition:

- All examples in this edition require at least tmux 3.4. Previous versions use different configuration syntax for some options or have different behavior.

- This book covers Windows 10 and 11 installation using the much more streamlined Windows Subsystem for Linux.

- Chapter 2, Configuring tmux, on page 15 now reflects the new configuration syntax introduced in tmux 3.

- Chapter 5, Pair Programming with tmux, on page 63 has an updated method for remote pairing, as the previous method is no longer compatible with tmux 3. You'll also find updated instructions for sharing sockets between users.

- Chapter 6, Workflows, on page 73 contains updates to existing workflows and introduces hooks, popup windows, and configurable menus.

In addition, you'll find smaller changes throughout the book to clarify explanations and add more context, all based on previous reader feedback.

What You'll Need

To use tmux, you'll need a computer that runs macOS, Windows 10 or 11 with WSL and Bash support or a flavor of Unix or Linux. Unfortunately, tmux doesn't run under the regular Windows Command Prompt or Powershell, but it will run great under WSL. You can also explore tmux on a virtual machine, VPS, cloud, or shared hosting environment running Linux or FreeBSD.

You should also have a good grasp of using command-line tools on a macOS, Linux, or Unix-like system. You'll use the Bash shell in this book, and being comfortable with creating directories and text files, as well as some basic scripting will help you move more quickly through the examples.

While not required, some experience with text editors such as Vim or Emacs might be helpful. tmux works in much the same way, and it has some predefined keyboard shortcuts that you may find familiar if you use one of these text editors.

Conventions

You drive tmux with the keyboard; you'll encounter many keyboard shortcuts throughout the book. Since tmux supports both lowercase and uppercase keyboard shortcuts, it may sometimes be unclear which key the book is referencing.

These are the conventions you'll find throughout the book:

- `Ctrl`-`b` means "press the `Ctrl` and `b` keys simultaneously."

- `Ctrl`-`R` means you'll press the `Ctrl` and `r` keys simultaneously, but you'll need to use the `Shift` key to produce the capital "R." I won't explicitly show the `Shift` key in any of these keystrokes.

- `Ctrl`-`b` `d` means "press the `Ctrl` and `b` keys simultaneously, then release, and then press `d`." In Chapter 1, Learning the Basics, on page 1, you'll learn about the *command prefix*, which will use this notation, but shortened to `Prefix` `d`.

- You'll find many terminal commands throughout the book, like this:

```
$ tmux new-session
```

The dollar sign represents the prompt from the Bash shell session. You won't need to type it when you type the command. It just denotes that this is a command you should type.

- Finally, as you'll see in Chapter 2, Configuring tmux, on page 15, you can configure tmux with a configuration file in your home directory called .tmux.conf. Filenames starting with a period don't show up in directory listings on most systems or text editors by default. Code listings in this book have a header that points to the file in the book's source code download, like this:

```
config/tmux.conf
# Set the prefix from C-b to C-a
set -g prefix C-a
```

To make it easier for you to find the file in the source code download, I've named the example file tmux.conf, without the leading period. The headers above the code listing reference that file.

Online Resources

The book's website[1] has links to submit errata for the book as well as the source code for the configuration files and scripts you'll use in this book. If you're reading the electronic copy of this book, you can click the filename above code excerpts to view the file's full source code. If you're reading the electronic copy of this book, you can click the filename above code excerpts to view the file's full source code. I also host a companion website for the book.[2]

Working with tmux has made me much more productive over the years, and the last two editions of this book helped thousands of developers put tmux to use for them. I'm excited to share this third edition with you. Let's get started by installing tmux and working with its basic features.

---

1. https://pragprog.com/titles/bhtmux3/tmux-3/
2. https://tmuxbook.com

## CHAPTER 1

Learning the Basics

tmux can be an incredible productivity booster once you get the hang of it. In this chapter, you'll get acquainted with tmux's basic features as you manage applications within sessions, windows, and panes. These simple concepts make up the foundation of what makes tmux an amazing environment for developers and system administrators alike.

But, before you can learn how to use these basic features, you need to get tmux installed.

Installing tmux

You can install tmux in one of two ways: using a package manager for your operating system, or building tmux from source.

Whichever method you choose, you'll want to ensure you install tmux version 3.4 or higher. Previous versions of tmux don't support some of the features you're going to explore in this book, or they have a configuration that's incompatible.

Installing on a Mac

The easiest way to install tmux on the Mac is with Homebrew.[1]

First, install the command-line tools Homebrew needs if you don't have them installed already. Open a new terminal and run the following command:

```
$ xcode-select --install
```

Next, install Homebrew by following the instructions on the Homebrew website.

---

1. http://brew.sh

Finally, install tmux with the following terminal command:

```
$ brew install tmux
```

To ensure that tmux is installed properly, and to check that you have the correct version, execute the following command from your terminal:

```
$ tmux -V
tmux 3.5a
```

With tmux installed, move on to Starting tmux, on page 3.

Installing on Windows

Windows has a feature called the Windows Subsystem for Linux, or WSL. When enabled, you're able to run a Linux distribution on Windows. This gives you access to a Bash shell which can run tmux. To use it, first ensure you're running Windows 10 version 2004 or higher, or Windows 11.

Install WSL by opening a new PowerShell prompt with Administrator access. At the prompt, enter the following command to install WSL and install the Ubuntu Linux distribution of Linux:

```
wsl --install
```

Once it finishes, you'll be prompted to create a user. You can use the same username as your Windows user or choose something completely different. This user account is separate from your regular Windows account; you'll only use it when you open a WSL prompt.

Once WSL is installed and your user is configured, move on to the next section, as you'll install tmux from source as if you were using Linux.

Installing on Linux

On Linux, your best bet is to install tmux by downloading the source code and compiling it yourself. Package managers don't always have the most recent version of tmux available. The process of installing tmux is the same on all platforms. You'll need the GCC compiler, and libevent and ncurses, which tmux depends on.

For Ubuntu-based systems, install all of tmux's dependencies with the apt package manager:

```
$ sudo apt install libevent-dev ncurses-dev build-essential bison pkg-config
```

With the compilers and prerequisites installed, grab the tmux source code and download it.[2] Untar the downloaded version and install it with the following commands:

```
$ tar -zxvf tmux-3.5a.tar.gz
$ cd tmux-3.5a
$ ./configure
$ make
$ sudo make install
```

You can test the installation by executing the following command from the terminal, which returns the currently installed version of tmux:

```
$ tmux -V
tmux 3.5a
```

Now that you have tmux properly installed, let's explore its core features, starting with a basic session.

Starting tmux

Starting tmux is as easy as typing tmux in your terminal:

```
$ tmux
```

You'll see something that looks like the following image appear on your screen.

This is a tmux "session," and it works just like your normal terminal session. You can issue any terminal command you'd like, and everything will work as

---

2.   https://tmux.github.io/

expected. Some programs might not display the right colors, but you'll address that in Configuring Support for Colors, on page 24.

At the bottom of the window is the status line. By default, it shows the tmux session number, the window index, the name of the program that's currently running, your host name, and the date and time. You can run multiple tmux sessions on your machine at the same time, and each session can have multiple windows, so the status line indicates where you are.

To close the tmux session, type exit in the session itself, or press Ctrl + d . This will close tmux and then return you to the standard terminal session

But, unless you're only using tmux for a brief period, this isn't the best way to work with sessions in tmux. You can instead create *named sessions* that you can then identify and work with later.

Creating Named Sessions

You can have multiple sessions on a single computer, and you'll want to be able to keep them organized. For example, you might have one session for each application you're developing or a session for work and a session for your cool side project. You can keep these sessions organized by giving each session you create its own unique name. Try it out right now. Create a named session called "basic" with the following command:

```
$ tmux new-session -s basic
```

You can shorten this command to this:

```
$ tmux new -s basic
```

When you enter this command, you'll be brought into a brand-new tmux session, but you won't really notice anything special or different than if you started things up normally. If you typed exit, you'd just be right back at the terminal. Named sessions come in handy when you want to leave tmux running in the background, which you'll explore shortly. But before you continue, close the session and exit tmux:

```
$ exit
```

Before you look at how to work with tmux sessions and run programs in the background, let's talk about how you send commands to tmux.

The Command Prefix

Since your command-line programs run inside tmux, you need a way to tell tmux that the command you're typing is meant for tmux and not for the

underlying application. The Ctrl - b combination does just that. This combination is called the *command prefix*.

You prefix each tmux command with this key combination. To get a feel for
how this works, open tmux again:

```
$ tmux
```

Then, inside of tmux, press Ctrl - b , then press t . A large clock will appear
on the screen.

It's important to note that you don't hold all these keys down together. Instead,
first press Ctrl - b simultaneously, release those keys, and then immediately
press the key for the command you want to send to tmux.

Throughout the rest of this book, I'll use the notation Prefix , followed by the
shortcut key for tmux commands, like Prefix t for showing the clock. In
Chapter 2, Configuring tmux, on page 15, you'll remap the prefix to a different
combination, but until then, you'll use the default of Ctrl - b whenever you
see Prefix .

Press the Enter key to dismiss the clock, and exit tmux by typing exit. Now,
let's look at how to run programs in the background.

Detaching and Attaching Sessions

One of tmux's biggest advantages is that you can fire it up, start up programs
or processes inside the tmux environment, and then leave everything running
in the background by "detaching" from the session.

If you close a regular terminal session, all the programs you have running in that session are killed off. But when you detach from a tmux session, you're not actually closing tmux. Any programs you started up in that session will stay running. You can then "attach" to the session and pick up where you left off.

To demonstrate this, create a new named tmux session, start up a program, and detach from the session. First, create the session:

```
$ tmux new -s basic
```

Then, within the tmux session, start an application called top, which monitors our memory and CPU usage, like this:

```
$ top
```

You'll have something that looks like the following figure running in your terminal.

```
top - 14:15:01 up 15 days, 11:43,  0 user,  load average: 0.05, 0.02, 0.00
Tasks:  11 total,   1 running,  10 sleeping,   0 stopped,   0 zombie
%Cpu(s):  0.0 us,  0.5 sy,  0.0 ni, 99.5 id,  0.0 wa,  0.0 hi,  0.0 si,  0.0 st
MiB Mem :   1895.6 total,    112.9 free,    289.4 used,   1586.2 buff/cache
MiB Swap:      0.0 total,      0.0 free,      0.0 used.   1606.2 avail Mem

  PID USER      PR  NI    VIRT    RES    SHR S  %CPU  %MEM     TIME+ COMMAND
    1 root      20   0   12052   7040   6144 S   0.0   0.4   0:00.02 sshd
  336 ted       20   0    5612   3500   2560 S   0.0   0.2   0:00.10 tmux: server
  337 ted       20   0    4720   3712   3200 S   0.0   0.2   0:00.00 bash
  364 ted       20   0    4720   3712   3200 S   0.0   0.2   0:00.00 bash
  491 root      20   0   15768   7152   5888 S   0.0   0.4   0:00.03 sshd
  502 brian     20   0   16028   6384   4736 S   0.0   0.3   0:00.06 sshd
  503 brian     20   0    4728   3712   3200 S   0.0   0.2   0:00.00 bash
  513 brian     20   0    5188   3072   2688 S   0.0   0.2   0:00.00 tmux: client
  515 brian     20   0    5820   3496   2560 S   0.0   0.2   0:00.26 tmux: server
  544 brian     20   0    4692   3712   3200 S   0.0   0.2   0:00.00 bash
  556 brian     20   0    9044   4992   2944 R   0.0   0.3   0:00.06 top




[0] 0:top*                                               "puzzles" 14:14 30-Sep-24
```

Now, detach from the tmux session by pressing `Prefix` `d`. This returns you to your regular terminal prompt. The tmux session is still running, and the top program is running inside of that session.

Now, let's look at how to get back into that tmux session you left running. But before you do, close your terminal program.

Reattaching to Existing Sessions

You've set up a tmux session, fired up a program inside the session, detached from it, and even closed your terminal program, but the tmux session is still chugging along, along with the top application you launched.

You can list existing tmux sessions using the following command:

```
$ tmux list-sessions
```

You can shorten the command to this:

```
$ tmux ls
```

Open a new terminal window and list the sessions. The command's output shows that there's one session currently running:

```
basic: 1 windows (created Fri Jun 14 06:34:45 2024)
```

The output of the command shows the tmux session name you provided when you created the session, and it shows the time you created it.

To attach to the session, use the attach keyword. If you only have one session running, you can use the following command:

```
$ tmux attach
```

Execute that and you'll be attached to the session again.

You can have more than one tmux session running, and you can switch between them. Detach from the basic session with Prefix d .

Now create a new tmux session in the background using the following command:

```
$ tmux new -s second_session -d
```

This command creates a new session, but the -d switch tells tmux not to attach to the session automatically.

Now list the sections, and you'll see two sessions running:

```
$ tmux ls
basic: 1 windows (created Fri Jun 14 06:34:45 2024)
second_session: 1 windows (created Fri Jun 14 06:38:37 2024)
```

You can attach to the session you want by using tmux attach with the -t flag, followed by the session name. Run the following command:

```
$ tmux attach -t second_session
```

This attaches you to the second_session tmux session. You can detach from this session just as you did previously, using Prefix d , and then attach to a different session. In Moving Between Sessions, on page 78, you'll see some other ways to move between active sessions.

Now let's remove the active sessions.

Killing Sessions

There are two ways to end a tmux session. First, you can attach to the session, stop all the programs within the session, and then type exit within a session. You can also kill off sessions with the kill-session command. It works just like tmux attach.

Run the following commands to end the basic and second_session sessions you created:

```
$ tmux kill-session -t basic
$ tmux kill-session -t second_session
```

If you list the sessions again, you will get a message telling you tmux is not running:

```
$ tmux ls
no server running on /tmp/tmux-1002/default
```

Since there are no tmux sessions running, tmux itself isn't running, so it isn't able to handle the request.

The tmux kill-session command is the equivalent of closing a terminal. All of the processes inside are killed. This command is incredibly useful for situations where a program in a session becomes unresponsive.

Now that you know the basics of creating and working with sessions, you'll look at how you can work with multiple programs within a single session.

Working with Windows

It's possible, and common, to run multiple, simultaneous commands within a tmux session. In fact, it's one of tmux's main advantages. You can keep these organized with windows, which are similar to tabs in modern graphical terminal emulators or web browsers.

When you create a new tmux session, the environment sets up an initial window for you. You can create as many as you'd like, and they will persist when you detach and reattach from the session.

To try this out, you'll create a new session that has two windows. The first window will have your normal shell prompt, and the second window will run the top command.

Create a named session called windows:

```
$ tmux new -s windows -n shell
```

By using the -n flag, you tell tmux to name the first window so you can identify it easily.

Next, you'll add a window to this session.

Creating and Naming Windows

To create a window in a current session, press `Prefix` `c`. Creating a window like this automatically brings the new window into focus. From here, you can start up another application. Start top in this new window:

```
$ top
```

The first window has a name you defined, called "shell," but the second window now appears to have the name "top." This window's name changes based on the app that's currently running because you never gave it a default name when you created it. So, let's give this window a proper name.

To rename a window, press `Prefix` followed by `,` (a comma), and the status line changes, letting you rename the current window. Rename the window to Processes.

You can create as many windows in a tmux session as you'd like. But once you have more than one, you need to be able to move between them.

Moving Between Windows

So far, you've created two windows in your environment, and you can navigate around these windows in several ways. When you only have two windows, you can quickly move between windows with `Prefix` `n`, for "next window." This cycles through the windows you have open. Since you only have two windows right now, this just toggles between them.

You can use `Prefix` `p` to go to the *previous* window.

By default, windows in tmux each have a number, starting at 0. You can quickly jump to the first window with `Prefix` `0`, and the second window with `Prefix` `1`. This zero-based array of windows isn't always intuitive, and in Chapter 2, Configuring tmux, on page 15, you'll see how to make the list of windows start at one instead of zero.

If you end up with more than nine windows, you can use `Prefix` `w` to display a visual menu of your windows so you can select the one you'd like. You can also use `Prefix` `f` to find a window that contains a string of text. Typing the text and pressing `Enter` displays a list of windows containing that text.

From here, you can continue creating new windows and launching programs. When you detach from your session and reattach later, your windows will all be where you left them.

To close a window, you can either type "exit" into the prompt in the window, or you can use `Prefix` `&`, which displays a confirmation message in the status bar before killing off the window. If you accept, your previous window comes into focus. To completely close out the tmux session, you have to close all the windows in the session.

Creating windows is great, but you can make tmux even more useful by splitting a window into panes.

Working with Panes

Having programs in separate windows is fine for programs you don't mind having out of the way. But with tmux, you can divide a single session into panes so you can run multiple programs on the screen at once.

Create a new tmux session called "panes" so you can experiment with how panes work. Exit any existing tmux sessions and create a new one like this:

```
$ tmux new -s panes
```

You can split windows vertically or horizontally. Let's split the window in half vertically first, and then horizontally, creating one large pane on the left and two smaller panes on the right, as shown in the following image:

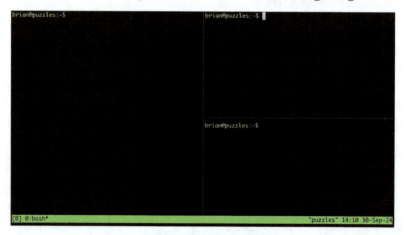

In the tmux session, press `Prefix` `%`, and the window will divide down the middle and start up a second terminal session in the new pane. In addition, the focus will move to this new pane.

Now press `Prefix` `"` (double quote) to split this new pane in half horizontally. By default, new panes split the existing pane in half evenly.

To cycle through the panes, press `Prefix` `o`. You can also use `Prefix`, followed by the `Up`, `Down`, `Left`, or `Right` keys to move around the panes.

With just a couple of keystrokes, you've divided one window into a workspace with three panes. Let's look at how you can rearrange these panes with layouts.

Pane Layouts

You can resize a pane, either using incremental resizing or by using templates. Resizing panes incrementally using the default keybindings is quite awkward. In Chapter 2, Configuring tmux, on page 15, you'll define some shortcuts to make resizing panes easier. For now, you'll use one of tmux's several default pane layouts:

- even-horizontal stacks all panes horizontally, left to right.

- even-vertical stacks all panes vertically, top to bottom.

- main-horizontal creates one larger pane on the top and smaller panes underneath.

- main-vertical creates one large pane on the left side of the screen, and stacks the rest of the panes vertically on the right.

- tiled arranges all panes evenly on the screen.

You can cycle through these layouts by pressing `Prefix` `Spacebar`.

Closing Panes

You close a pane the same way you exit a terminal session or a tmux window: you type "exit" in the pane. You can also kill a pane with `Prefix` `x`, which also closes the window if there's only one pane in that window.

tmux will prompt you to confirm that you want to kill the specified pane. Killing a pane like this is great for situations where the program running within the pane has gotten stuck, or you can't interact with it anymore.

So far, you've created new sessions, windows, and panes, and you've moved around a bit. Before you move on to more advanced topics, you'll explore some additional tmux commands by using Command mode.

Working with Command Mode

So far, you've used key combinations to create windows and panes, but those keybindings are actually just shortcuts for tmux commands with some preset options.

You can execute tmux commands two ways: from the terminal itself or from the command area in the tmux status line. You'll learn about using tmux commands from the terminal in Chapter 3, Scripting Customized tmux Environments, on page 41, but for now, you'll get comfortable with tmux's Command mode by using it to create some new windows and panes in a currently running workspace.

To enter Command mode, press `Prefix` `:` (the colon) from within a running tmux session. The status line changes color, and you get a prompt that indicates that you can type your command.

Create a new window by using the new-window command, like this:

```
new-window -n console
```

By using a command rather than the shortcut, you can create a new window and give it a name at the same time by using the -n flag. Let's take this a step further and launch a new window that starts the top program. To do that, enter Command mode and type this command:

```
new-window -n processes "top"
```

Command Mode supports tab-completion for tmux commands, so you can save a few keystrokes when entering commands.

When you press `Enter`, a new window appears and the top application runs, showing your running processes.

Specifying an initial command for a window is extremely handy for short-term tasks, but there's a slight wrinkle. If you exit the top app by pressing `q`, the tmux window you created will also close. You can use configuration settings to get around this, but if you want the window to persist, create the window without specifying an initial command, and then execute your own command in the new window.

You can use Command mode to create new windows, new panes, or new sessions, or even set other environmental options. In Chapter 2, Configuring tmux, on page 15, you'll create a few custom keybindings to make some of these commands easier to use.

What's Next?

In this chapter, you explored basic usage of tmux sessions, panes, windows, and commands, but there's a lot more you can try.

By pressing ⎡Prefix⎤ ⎡?⎤, you can get a list of all predefined tmux keybindings and the associated commands these trigger.

As you work with tmux, think about how you can create different environments for your work. If you're monitoring servers, you could use tmux panes to create a dashboard that shows your various monitoring scripts and log files.

With the basics under your belt, you'll now put together a custom configuration you can use for the rest of your work.

For Future Reference

Creating Sessions

Command	Description
tmux new-session	Creates a new session without a name. Can be shortened to tmux new or tmux
tmux new -s development	Creates a new session called "development"
tmux new -s development -n editor	Creates a session named "development" and names the first window "editor"
tmux attach -t development	Attaches to a session named "development"

Default Commands for Sessions, Windows, and Panes

Command	Description
Prefix d	Detaches from the session, leaving the session running in the background
Prefix :	Enters Command mode
Prefix c	Creates a new window from within an existing tmux session. Shortcut for new-window
Prefix n	Moves to the next window
Prefix p	Moves to the previous window
Prefix 0 ... 9	Selects windows by number
Prefix w	Displays a selectable list of windows in the current session

Command	Description
Prefix f	Searches for a window that contains the text you specify. Displays a selectable list of windows containing that text in the current session
Prefix ,	Displays a prompt to rename a window
Prefix &	Closes the current window after prompting for confirmation
Prefix %	Divides the current window in half vertically
Prefix "	Divides the current window in half horizontally
Prefix o	Cycles through open panes
Prefix q	Momentarily displays pane numbers in each pane
Prefix x	Closes the current pane after prompting for confirmation
Prefix Space	Cycles through the various pane layouts

Configuring tmux

tmux, by default, doesn't have the most friendly commands. Many of the most important and useful features are assigned to hard-to-reach keystrokes or consist of long, verbose command strings. Also, tmux's default color scheme isn't very easy on the eyes. In this chapter, you'll build a basic configuration file for your environment that you'll then use for the rest of this book. You'll start out by customizing how you navigate around the screen and how you create and resize panes, and then you'll explore some more advanced settings. You'll also make sure your terminal is properly configured so the visual settings you'll make to tmux's appearance display the correct colors. When you're done, you'll have a better understanding of how flexible tmux is, and you can start making it your own. Let's start by talking about how to configure tmux in the first place.

Introducing the .tmux.conf File

By default, tmux looks for configuration settings in a few places. It first looks in /etc/tmux.conf for a system-wide configuration. It then looks in the user's home directory for the file .config/tmux/tmux.conf. tmux also looks in $XDG_CONFIG_HOME/tmux/, which is usually $HOME/.config/tmux, but is user-configurable. It finally looks for a file called .tmux.conf in the current user's home directory. If none of these files exist, tmux uses its default settings.

You don't need to create a system-wide configuration, so you'll create a configuration file in your home directory. Execute the following command in your shell to create the file .tmux.conf in your home directory:

```
$ touch ~/.tmux.conf
```

In this file, you can do everything from defining new key shortcuts to setting up a default environment with multiple windows, panes, and running programs. Let's start by setting a couple of basic options that will make working with tmux much easier.

 The .tmux.conf file is a hidden file and doesn't show up in file explorers or directory listings by default. The labels above the code listings in this book reference the file as tmux.conf, without the leading period, so it corresponds with the file in the book's source code download.

Defining an Easier Prefix

As you saw earlier, tmux uses `Ctrl`-`b` as its command prefix. Many tmux users started out using GNU-Screen, which uses `Ctrl`-`a` for its command prefix. `Ctrl`-`a` is an excellent choice for a prefix because it's easier to trigger, especially if you remap your computer's `Caps Lock` key to `Ctrl` as explained in the sidebar that follows. This keeps your hands on the home row of your keyboard.

Remapping the Caps Lock Key

On many keyboards, the `Caps Lock` key sits right next to the `a` key on the home row of the keyboard. By remapping this key to `Ctrl`, you can make triggering commands more comfortable.

On your Mac, you can remap the `Caps Lock` key under the Keyboard preference pane, under System Preferences. Just press the Modifier Keys button and change the action for `Caps Lock` to "Control."

On Linux, the process depends on your distribution and window manager, but you can find several methods described on the Emacs wiki. [a]

This small change to your configuration can save you a surprising amount of time over the course of a day.

_____

a.   http://www.emacswiki.org/emacs/MovingTheCtrlKey

To set options in the .tmux.conf file, use the set-option command, which you can shorten to set. You define the tmux prefix by adding this to the .tmux.conf file:

config/tmux.conf
```
# Set the prefix from C-b to C-a
set -g prefix C-a
```

In this example, you're using the -g switch, for "global," which sets the option for all tmux sessions you create. While they're global, you can override these options later.

The line starting with # is a comment. It's a good idea to put comments in your configuration files; they'll jog your memory later on when you go back and look at your configuration a few months from now. Comments in a tmux configuration file work just like comments in source code.

You use the unbind-key, or unbind command, to remove a keybinding that's been defined so you can assign a different command to this key later. Free up Ctrl - b by adding the following to your configuration file:

config/tmux.conf
```
# Free the original Ctrl-b prefix keybinding
unbind C-b
```

tmux won't see changes you make to your file automatically. So, if you're editing your .tmux.conf file while tmux is running, you'll either need to completely close *all* tmux sessions, or enter tmux's Command mode with Prefix : and type the following command whenever you make a change:

```
source-file ~/.tmux.conf
```

You can now use Ctrl - a for your prefix. The rest of the examples in this book will continue to refer to it as Prefix , though.

Changing the Default Delay

tmux adds a very small delay when sending commands, and this delay can interfere with other programs such as the Vim text editor. You can set this delay so these programs become much more responsive. Add the following line to your configuration file to set a smaller delay:

```
# Set the delay between prefix and command
set -s escape-time 1
```

The -s flag sets tmux Server options, which apply to the entire tmux server and all sessions it manages. The difference between -s and -g is that when you use -s to set options, you can't override them in a specific session later.

Once you reload the configuration file, you'll be able to issue keystrokes without delay.

Setting the Window and Panes Index

In Chapter 1, Learning the Basics, on page 1, you saw that when you create more than one window in a session, you can reference windows by their index. This index starts at zero, which can be a little awkward since you'd have to use Prefix 0 to access the first window. Add the following line to your configuration file to make the window index start at 1:

```
# Set the base index for windows to 1 instead of 0
set -g base-index 1
```

New tmux sessions will have this setting applied automatically, but your current session won't. You'll have to close the session and restart it. Once you do, you can use Prefix 1 to jump to the first window. That's a lot easier since the keys on the keyboard now directly correspond with the windows listed in the status line.

You can also set the starting index for panes using the pane-base-index option. Add this line to your configuration so you have some consistency between pane and window numbering:

config/tmux.conf
```
# Set the base index for panes to 1 instead of 0
set -w -g pane-base-index 1
```

Up until now, you've used the set -g command, which sets global options for the tmux session. The set command lets you set options for windows and panes as well. The pane-base-index option is a window option, so you should add the -w flag. If you leave it off, tmux will still figure out what you mean, but it's best to be explicit in case that behavior changes.

Now, let's build some useful shortcuts that will increase your productivity.

Customizing Keys, Commands, and User Input

Many of the default keyboard shortcuts in tmux are a bit of a stretch, both physically and mentally. Not only is Prefix % hard to press, as it involves holding three keys, but without looking at the command reference, there's no easy way to remember what it does.

In this section, you'll define, or redefine, some of the most-used tmux commands. You'll start by creating a custom keybinding to reload the tmux configuration.

Creating a Shortcut to Reload the Configuration

Every time you make a change to your configuration file, you either have to shut down *all* sessions and then restart tmux, or issue the source command to reload your configuration from within the running instances. Let's create a custom keybinding to reload the configuration file.

The bind-key command, or bind for short, defines a new keybinding. You specify the key you want to use, followed by the command you want to perform.

Define Prefix r so it reloads the .tmux.conf file in the current session. Add this line to your configuration file:

```
bind r source-file ~/.tmux.conf
```

When you define keybindings this way, you still have to push the Prefix key before you can press the newly defined key. And while you just defined a new command to make reloading the tmux configuration easier, you can't use it until you reload the configuration file. So, be sure to enter Command mode with Prefix : and reload the file manually one more time:

```
source-file ~/.tmux.conf
```

When you reload the file, you might not always be able to tell that anything changed, but you can use the display command to put a message in the status line. Modify your reload command to display the text Configuration reloaded when the configuration file loads:

```
# Reload the file with Prefix r
bind r source-file ~/.tmux.conf \; display-message "Configuration reloaded"
```

As you can see, you can bind a key to a series of commands by separating the commands with the \; character combination.

There's a lot going on with that command, so to improve readability, you can put the command on multiple lines. To do so, place the \ character after part of the command, and continue the command on the next line:

```
config/tmux.conf
# Reload the file with Prefix r
bind r \
    source-file ~/.tmux.conf \; \
    display-message "Configuration reloaded"
```

The \ character has to be the last thing on each line, and you can't place it within a string. You can indent the next line to improve readability. In Chapter 6, Workflows, on page 73, some of the commands get longer, so you'll see this approach a few times in that chapter.

With this keybinding in place, you can make additional changes to the configuration file and then immediately activate them by pressing Prefix r.

> ### Defining Keybindings That Don't Require a Prefix
>
> Using the bind command with the -n prefix tells tmux that the keybinding doesn't require pressing the prefix. For example, the following definition would make Ctrl - r reload the configuration file:
>
> ```
> bind-key -n C-r source-file ~/.tmux.conf
> ```
>
> Unfortunately, this would completely disable that key combination in any application that's running in a tmux session. You'll want to use this with care.

Sending the Prefix to Other Applications

You've remapped Ctrl - a as the Prefix, but programs such as Vim, Emacs, and even the regular Bash shell also use that combination. You'll want to configure tmux to send that command through when you need it. You can do that by binding the send-prefix command to a keystroke.

Add the following line to your configuration file:

```
# Ensure that we can send Ctrl-A to other apps
bind C-a send-prefix
```

After reloading the configuration file, you can send Ctrl - a to an application running within tmux simply by pressing Ctrl - a twice.

Define New Keys for Splitting Panes

The default keys for splitting panes are difficult to remember, so you'll set your own keys that you won't be able to forget. You'll set the horizontal split to Prefix | and the vertical split to Prefix -. To do that, add these lines to your configuration:

```
config/tmux.conf
# Split panes with | and -
bind | split-window -h
bind - split-window -v
```

At first glance, this may look backward. The -v and -h flags on split-window stand for "vertical" and "horizontal" splits, but to tmux, a vertical split means creating a new pane below the existing pane so the panes are stacked vertically on top of each other. A horizontal split means creating a new pane *next* to the existing one so the panes are stacked horizontally across the screen. So, in order to divide the window vertically, you use a "horizontal" split, and to divide it horizontally, you use a "vertical" split.

These new shortcuts give you a nice visual association. If you want your windows split, you press the key that looks like the split you want to create.

Remapping Movement Keys

Moving from pane to pane with Prefix o is cumbersome, and using the arrow keys means you have to take your fingers off the home row. If you use the Vim text editor, you're probably familiar with its use of h, j, k, and l for movement keys. You can remap the movement keys in tmux to these same keys. Add the following lines to your configuration file to map those keys:

```
# Move between panes with Prefix h,j,k,l
bind h select-pane -L
bind j select-pane -D
bind k select-pane -U
bind l select-pane -R
```

In addition, you can use Prefix Ctrl-h and Prefix Ctrl-l to cycle through the windows by binding those keystrokes to the respective commands by adding these lines:

```
bind C-h select-window -t :-
bind C-l select-window -t :+
```

Reload your configuration file. Provided you've mapped your Caps Lock key to the Ctrl key, you can now move between panes without moving your hands off the home row.

Define Keys to Resize Panes

To resize a pane, you can enter Command mode and type resize-pane -D to resize a pane downward one row at a time. You can increase the resizing increment by passing a number after the direction, such as resize-pane -D 5. The command itself is pretty verbose, but you can make some keybindings to make resizing panes easier.

To make it easier to remember, use a variation of the Vim movement keys to resize windows. Use Prefix H, Prefix J, Prefix K, and Prefix L to change the size of the panes. Add these lines to your configuration file:

```
bind H resize-pane -L 5
bind J resize-pane -D 5
bind K resize-pane -U 5
bind L resize-pane -R 5
```

Notice that you're using uppercase letters in the configuration file. tmux allows both lowercase and uppercase letters for keystrokes. You'll need to use the Shift key to trigger the uppercase keystroke.

Using these movement keys will help you keep track of which way you want the window size to change. For example, you may have a window divided into two panes stacked vertically, like this:

If you want to increase the size of Pane 1, then you'd place your cursor inside Pane 1 and then press `Prefix` `J`, which moves the horizontal divider *downward*. If you pressed `Prefix` `K`, tmux would move the horizontal divider up.

With the configuration you just used, you have to press the `Prefix` each time you want to resize the pane. But if you use the -r flag with the `bind` command, you can specify that you want the key to be *repeatable*, meaning you can press the prefix key only once and then continuously press the defined key within a given window of time, called the repeat limit.

Redefine the window resizing commands by adding the -r option:

```
# Pane resizing panes with Prefix H,J,K,L
bind -r H resize-pane -L 5
bind -r J resize-pane -D 5
bind -r K resize-pane -U 5
bind -r L resize-pane -R 5
```

Now you can resize the panes by pressing `Prefix` `J` once, and then press `J` until the window is the size you want. The default repeat limit is 500 milliseconds, and can be changed by setting the repeat-time option to a higher value.

You can also update the keybindings to switch windows to use the -r flag:

```
# Quick window selection
bind -r C-h select-window -t :-
bind -r C-l select-window -t :+
```

This will let you press `Prefix` `Ctrl`-`l` once, and then you can keep pressing `Ctrl`-`l` to move through your windows.

Next, you'll look at how tmux works with your mouse.

> **Joe asks:**
> ## Can I See a List of Keybindings?
>
> tmux comes with many existing keybindings, so when you want to define your own, you might not know what's available. To get a list of each keybinding and its associated command, press `Prefix` `?`, to see a list of default tmux keybindings and explanations of what they do.
>
> The list of keybindings appears, and you can scroll through the list with the arrow keys or press `esc` to dismiss the list.
>
> This list doesn't show any of the custom keybindings you create, so enter Command mode with `Prefix` `:` and enter the following command to see all of the keybindings and the associated commands:
>
> ```
> list-keys
> ```
>
> You can use this list to verify you've set your keybindings correctly or check what keybindings already exist so that you can unbind them and use the key combination for something else.

Handling the Mouse

While tmux is meant to be completely keyboard-driven, there are times when you may find it easier to use the mouse. If your terminal is set up to forward mouse clicks and movement through to programs in the terminal, then you can tell tmux how to handle certain mouse events.

Sometimes, it's nice to be able to scroll up through the terminal buffer with the mouse wheel or to select windows and panes, especially when you're just getting started with tmux. To configure tmux so you can use the mouse, you need to enable mouse mode.

```
set -g mouse on
```

This setting configures tmux so it will let you use the mouse to select a pane or resize a pane, let you click the window list to select a window, or even let you use the mouse to scroll backward through the buffer if your terminal supports it.

This can be a handy addition to your configuration, but remember that using the mouse with tmux will slow you down. Even though being able to scroll and click might seem like a neat idea, you should learn the keyboard equivalents for switching panes and moving forward and backward through the buffers. So, for your configuration file, disable the mouse. Add the following line to do that:

config/tmux.conf
```
# Mouse support - set to on if you want to use the mouse
set -g mouse off
```

Setting this option prevents you from accidentally doing things when you select the terminal window with your mouse. It also forces you to get more comfortable with the keyboard. If you decide that you do want to use the mouse anyway, you can toggle it back on.

The flexible configuration system tmux provides lets you customize the way you interact with the interface, but you can also configure its appearance to make its interface easier to see, and in some cases, more informative.

Changing How tmux Looks

tmux provides quite a few ways to customize your environment's appearance. In this section, you'll configure some of these options as you customize the status line and other components. You'll start by configuring the colors for various elements, and then you'll turn your bland status line into something that will provide you with some vital information about your environment.

Configuring Support for Colors

To get the best visual experience out of tmux, make sure that both your terminal and tmux are configured for 256 colors.

Using the tput command, you can quickly determine the number of colors supported by your terminal session. Enter the following command in your terminal:

```
$ tput colors
256
```

If you don't see 256 as the result, you'll need to do a little configuration.

You may need to configure your terminal to use xterm's 256 mode. On the Mac, you can configure this in the Terminal app by editing the profile as shown in the following figure:

If you're using iTerm2,[1] you can find this by editing the default profile and changing the terminal mode to xterm-256color:

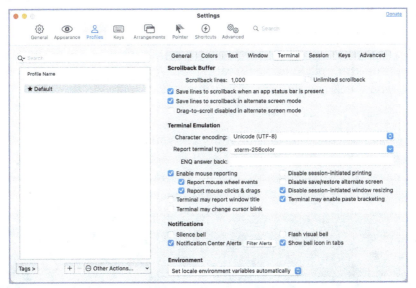

If you're using Linux, you might need to modify your shell configuration files to enable a 256-color terminal. Add this line to your .bashrc file if you're using the Bash shell, or add it to your .zshrc file if you're using zsh as your shell:

```
[ -z "$TMUX_PANE" ] && export TERM=xterm-256color
```

This conditional statement ensures that the TERM variable is only set outside of tmux, since tmux sets its own value for TERM. Be sure to close and reopen your terminal to ensure the changes take effect.

Also, ensure that your terminal emulator supports displaying UTF-8 characters so that visual elements such as the pane dividers appear as dashed lines.

To ensure that tmux displays things in 256 colors, add this line to your .tmux.conf file so that tmux reports a 256-color terminal to other programs:

config/tmux.conf
```
# Set the default terminal mode to 256color mode
set -g default-terminal "tmux-256color"
```

To make this change take effect, you'll have to stop all running tmux sessions.

If you're on macOS, or you notice some programs don't display colors correctly, this may be because some programs you're using are outdated and don't recognize the tmux-256color terminal configuration. These programs, like tmux,

---

1.   http://www.iterm2.com

rely on a library called ncurses to display colors. This is a common issue on macOS because macOS itself ships with a very old version of ncurses and that version is what its built-in commands like man, ls and other tools use. Programs you install with Homebrew will work fine, as those use a newer version of ncurses.

Fixing this is beyond the scope of this book as it involves either updating all of the outdated applications or creating and maintaining your own terminal profile. The quick solution is to use screen-256color instead, like this:

```
set -g default-terminal "screen-256color"
```

Once you've set the right terminal profile, you'll find it much easier to use programs such as Vim, Emacs, and other full-color programs from within tmux, especially when you are using more complex color schemes for syntax highlighting. Take a look at the following image to see the difference:

The Vim instance on the left is only using 16 colors, whereas the instance on the right uses 256 colors. The colors on the right are more readable, and the background is lighter.

Next, you'll configure the appearance of tmux's components, starting with colors.

Changing Colors

You can change the colors of several parts of the tmux interface, including the status line, window list, message area, and even the pane borders.

tmux provides variables you can use to specify colors, including black, red, green, yellow, blue, magenta, cyan, or white. You can also use colour0 to colour255 to reference more specific colors on the 256-color palette. You can also use color if you'd prefer that spelling; tmux supports both.

To find the numbers for those colors, you can run the following shell script to get the color variable you'd like to use:[2]

```
for i in {0..255} ; do
  printf "\x1b[38;5;${i}m${i} "
done
```

---

2. http://superuser.com/questions/285381/how-does-the-tmux-color-palette-work

Joe asks:
Can I Use 24-Bit Color with tmux?

Yes, if your terminal supports it. macOS's built-in terminal does not, but iTerm2 does, and many other modern terminals do as well. But you may also have to make changes to your tmux configuration file.

You can check to see if truecolor or RGB is available in tmux by running the following command within a tmux session:

```
$ tmux info | grep -e RGB -e Tc
```

If you see this output, your tmux session doesn't support RGB color:

```
197: RGB: [missing]
223: Tc: [missing]
```

To fix this, add the following line to your configuration file:

config/tmux.conf
```
# Override terminal so it displays 32bit RGB color
set -a terminal-overrides ",*256col*:RGB"
```

Then, restart tmux and check again. This time, you'll see that RGB is enabled:

```
197: RGB: (flag) true
223: Tc: [missing]
```

You can now use even more colors in your tmux sessions. You can test out 24-bit color support by running the truecolors.sh in the config folder in the book's companion files inside of your tmux session.

When you execute this command, you'll see the following output in your terminal, displaying the colors:

If your terminal supports 24-bit RGB color, you can specify colors using the same hex codes you'd use in CSS or by using RGB values. In this book, you'll use color names or stick to the 256 color palette.

tmux has specific configuration options for changing foreground and background colors for each of its components. Let's start exploring these by customizing the colors of the status line.

Changing the Status Line Colors

The default status line has black text on a bright green background. It's pretty bland, and depending on your terminal configuration, it can be hard to read. Let's make it have white text on a black background by default, so it looks like this:

```
[0] 1:bash*                                          "puzzles" 22:57 30-Sep-24
```

The status-style option sets the foreground and background colors of the status line as well as the style. Add the following line to your configuration to set the status line colors:

config/tmux.conf
```
# Set the status line's colors
set -g status-style fg=white,bg=black
```

You can set the foreground color and the background color, and you can control the appearance of the text, depending on whether or not your terminal supports it. As you can probably guess, the fg option sets the foreground color, and the bg option sets the background color.

This command supports the options dim, bright (or bold), reverse, underscore, blink, and italics, in addition to colors. For example, to make the status line's text white and bold, you'd use the following configuration:

```
set -g status-style fg=white,bold,bg=black
```

If you're not using the tmux-256color terminal profile inside of tmux, italics won't work.

You can also customize the colors of the items within the status line. Let's start by customizing the window list.

Changing the Window List Colors

tmux displays a list of windows in the status line. Let's make it more apparent which window is active by styling the active window red and the inactive windows cyan. The option window-status-style controls how regular windows look, and the window-status-current-style option controls how the active window looks. To configure the colors, you use the same syntax you used for the status-style option.

Let's make the names of the windows cyan, like this:

```
[0] 1:bash*                                          "puzzles" 22:59 30-Sep-24
```

Add this to your configuration file:

config/tmux.conf
```
# Set the color of the window list
set -g window-status-style fg=cyan,bg=black
```

You can use default for a value so it inherits from the color of the status line.

To style the active window with a red background and bold white text, add this to your configuration file:

```
# Set colors for the active window
set -g window-status-current-style fg=white,bold,bg=red
```

Now, inactive windows are cyan, and the active window is easily identifiable:

```
[0] 1:bash- 2:bash*                                  "puzzles" 23:00 30-Sep-24
```

This takes care of the window list. Next, you'll customize how panes within a window appear.

Changing the Appearance of Panes

tmux has several options to control how panes look. You can control the color of the pane dividers, you can define colors to make the active pane more apparent, and you can "dim out" the inactive panes. You can even give panes their own status lines.

Panes have both foreground and background colors. The foreground color of a pane is the actual dashed line that makes up the border. The background color, by default, is black, but if you color it when the pane is active, you can make the active pane extremely noticeable, as shown in the image on page 30.

Add this to your configuration file to add this effect to your environment:

config/tmux.conf
```
# Colors for pane borders
set -w -g pane-border-style fg=green,bg=black
set -w -g pane-active-border-style fg=black,bg=yellow
```

You can also control the border lines themselves. You can have a single line, a double line, or even use the pane's number. Add the following to your configuration to specify a single line border for your panes:

```
# Pane border style: single, double, heavy, simple, number.
set -w -g pane-border-lines single
```

Play with the options. You can choose single, double, heavy, simple, or number. The double and heavy options require UTF-8 support, so if you don't have that configured in your terminal, you won't see anything happen, as they'll fall back to standard characters.

When you only have two panes, tmux only highlights half of the active pane:

To make the active pane more clear, you can tell tmux to add an arrow that points to the active pane by adding this to your configuration file:

```
# Add indicators for two-pane setup
set -g pane-border-indicators arrows
```

This has the benefit of also applying the active color to the whole pane.

In addition, your panes can also have status lines. These status lines replace the bottom or top border of your pane's border with a status line displaying the pane number and the host:

```
─1 "puzzles"───────────────────────────────────────
To run a command as administrator (user "root"), use "sudo <command>".
See "man sudo_root" for details.

brian@puzzles:~$ vim .tmux.conf
brian@puzzles:~$




─2 "puzzles"───────────────────────────────────────
To run a command as administrator (user "root"), use "sudo <command>".
See "man sudo_root" for details.

brian@puzzles:~$
```

To turn this feature on, add this to your configuration:

```
# Add status to panes
set -g pane-border-status top
```

Finally, you may want to be able to more easily determine what the active pane is by changing the color of the foreground or background of the current pane. Or, you might want to fade out panes that are not in use. The window-style and window-active-style options let you control the foreground and background colors, although you have to specify both the foreground and background colors as part of the value you set for the option.

Let's dim out any pane that's not active. You achieve this by dimming all of the panes and then making the active pane look normal. Add these lines to your configuration:

```
# Active pane normal, other shaded out
set -g window-style fg=color240,bg=color235
set -g window-active-style fg=white,bg=black
```

To create the dimming effect, you set the foreground text color to a lighter grey, and then use a darker grey for the background color. Then, for the active window, you use black and white.

With this change and the active pane borders, it will be more clear which pane is active as shown in the image on page 32.

Next, you'll touch up the area of tmux where you issue commands.

Customizing the tmux Message Area

You can also customize the message area where you enter tmux commands and see alert messages. The approach is almost identical to the way you styled the status line itself.

To make the message area stand out from the status bar and other message areas in programs like Vim, which has its own message area, change the background color to a dark grey color and the text color to white. Use a bright white so the message stands out in more detail. Add this to your configuration:

config/tmux.conf
```
# Command / message line
set -g message-style fg=white,bg=color242,bold
```

This configuration uses a more specific color from the 256-color palette rather than a named color. You can mix and match color names, hex codes, and colors from the hex palette in a single command.

Reload the file to see the changes. If you used the reloading shortcut you created, you'll notice the changes right away when the "Configuration Reloaded" message appears. If you missed it, press Prefix : to enter command mode and you'll see the new colors applied.

Now that you've changed some colors, you'll change the information displayed in the status line on both sides of the window list.

Customizing the Status Line's Content

The tmux status line can display nearly any information you want. You can use some predefined components or create your own by executing shell commands and pulling in the results.

The status line consists of three components: a left panel, the window list, and a right panel. By default, it looks like this:

```
[development] 0:bash*                          "example.local" 13:37 14-Jun-24
```

On the left side, you have the name of the tmux session followed by the list of windows. The list of windows shows the numerical index of the current window and its name. On the right side, you have the host name of your computer followed by the date and time. Now, let's customize the content of the status line.

Configuring Status Line Items

You can change the content in the left or right panels of the status bar using a combination of text and variables. The following table shows some of the most useful variables you can use in your status line.

Variable	Description
host or #H	Hostname of local host
host_short or #h	Hostname of local host without the domain name
window_flags or #F	Current window flag
window_index or #I	Current window index
pane_index or #P	Current pane index
session_name or #S	Current session name
pane_title or #T	Current pane title
window_name or #W	Current window name
pid	tmux process ID
version	tmux version
##	A literal #
#(shell-command)	First line of the shell command's output
#[attributes]	Color or attribute change

Table 1—Status Line Variables

For example, if you wanted to show just the name of the current tmux session on the left, you'd use the set -g status-left option with the #S value, like this:

```
set -g status-left "#S"
```

But you can also make it stand out more by using an attribute to set the foreground color, like this:

```
set -g status-left "#[fg=green]#S"
```

You can add as many attributes and items to the status line as you want. Try this out by altering the left side of the status line so it shows the session name in green, the current window number in yellow, and the current pane in cyan. Add this line to your configuration file:

```
set -g status-left "#[fg=green]#S #[fg=yellow]#I #[fg=cyan]#P"
```

You can add any arbitrary text into the status line, too. Add text to make the session, window, and pane more noticeable, like this:

config/tmux.conf
```
# Status line left side to show Session: [name] [window] [pane]
set -g status-left-length 40
set -g status-left "#[fg=green]Session: #S #[fg=yellow]#I #[fg=cyan]#P"
```

This sets the status-left-length option because the specified output is too long for the default length, so you have to make that region wider. Your status line now looks like the following image:

You can configure the right side of the status line too. Add the current date and time with the following line::

config/tmux.conf
```
# Status line right side -  31-Oct 13:37
set -g status-right "#[fg=cyan]%d %b %R"
```

This formats the date as "Day-Month HH:SS," but you can format it however you'd like using the standard strftime() time formatting mechanism used in many programming languages. You can use foragoodstrftime.com[3] to help you find the perfect time format. Reload your configuration and your status line shows the new format:

You can also incorporate shell commands into the mix by using the #(shell-command) variable to return the result of any external command-line program into the status line. You'll do this in Adding Battery Life to the Status Line, on page 84.

---

3.   https://www.foragoodstrftime.com/

If you've enabled status lines for your panes, you can use the pane-border-format option to customize the pane status line using the same approach.

Centering the Window List

You can also control the placement of the window list. By default, the window list is left-aligned, but you can center the window list in between the left and right status areas with a single configuration change. Add this line to your configuration:

```
config/tmux.conf
# Center the window list in the status line
set -g status-justify centre
```

Save and refresh your configuration, and the window list appears centered:

```
Session: 0 2 1              1:bash-  2:bash*              30 Sep 23:46
```

As you create new windows, the window list will shift accordingly, staying in the center of the status line.

Keeping Status Line Info Up to Date

You've added the current time and some other dynamic information to your status line. By default, tmux refreshes the status line every 15 seconds, which is a reasonable default.

You can specify exactly how quickly tmux refreshes its status line with set -g status-interval, followed by the refresh interval in seconds. Add the following line to refresh the status line every 60 seconds.

```
# Update the status line every sixty seconds
set -g status-interval 60
```

Keep in mind that if you're firing off shell commands as part of your status bar, those will be executed once per interval, so be careful not to load too many resource-intensive scripts.

Identifying Activity in Other Windows

When you are working with more than one window, you will want to be notified when something happens in one of the other windows in your session so you can react to it. You can do that by adding a visual notification.

The monitor-activity on command highlights the window name in the status line when there's activity in that window. The visual-activity on line tells tmux to show a message in the status line as well. Add the following line to configure those options:

```
config/tmux.conf
# Enable activity alerts
set -w -g monitor-activity on
set -w -g visual-activity on
```

Reload your configuration file. Now, when one of the other windows has some activity, it'll stand out with a cyan background, like the top window shown in the following image:

Once you switch to that window, the colors will revert back to normal. If you want to configure different colors, you can do so with set -w -g window-status-activity-style and the colors of your choice.

Using Customize Mode

You've explored some of the more common configuration options, but there are many more tweaks you can make. Using the "customize mode," you can view and change many of the settings and key bindings for the active pane and window.

To access this mode, press Prefix : to enter the tmux command prompt and then type customize-mode or press Prefix C. The current pane will be replaced with an interface that shows the options:

Use the up and down arrow keys to navigate the interface and use the left and right arrow keys to expand and collapse the sections. The bottom pane shows a description of the option along with any notes.

Changing values in this mode will not save them to your configuration file, but this is a good way to explore the available options and experiment.

What's Next?

You've built up a solid configuration file throughout this chapter. Look at Appendix 1, Your Configuration, on page 95 to see the whole .tmux.conf file.

You can define additional options in your .tmux.conf file. For example, in Chapter 3, Scripting Customized tmux Environments, on page 41, you'll set up a custom default work environment using project-specific configuration files.

In addition, you can configure a default configuration for your system in /etc/tmux.conf. This is great for situations where you've set up a shared server so members of your team can collaborate or if you just want to ensure that every user on the system has some sensible defaults.

Now that you have a configuration defined, you'll create your own custom development environments with scripts so you can take advantage of tmux's panes and windows without having to set them up every day.

For Future Reference

Keybindings defined in this chapter

Command	Description
Ctrl - a	The new Prefix
Prefix a	Sends Ctrl - a to the program running in a tmux window or pane
Prefix r	Reloads the tmux configuration file
Prefix |	Splits the window horizontally
Prefix -	Splits the window vertically
Prefix h, Prefix j, Prefix k, and Prefix l	Moves between panes
Prefix H, Prefix J, Prefix K, and Prefix L	Resizes the current pane
Prefix Ctrl - h and Prefix Ctrl - l	Moves forward and backward through windows

Commands to control tmux's behavior

Command	Description
set-option [flags] [option] [value]	Sets options for sessions. Using the -g flag sets the option for all sessions. Using the -w flag sets options for windows. You can shorten this to set.
set -g prefix C-a	Sets the key combination for the Prefix key
set -s escape-time n	Sets the amount of time (in milliseconds) tmux waits for a keystroke after pressing Prefix
set -g base-index 1	Sets the base index for windows to 1 instead of 0
set -g pane-base-index 1	Sets the base index for panes to 1 instead of 0
source-file [file]	Loads a configuration file. Use this to reload the existing configuration or bring in additional configuration options later.
bind-key [key] [command]	Creates a keybinding that executes the specified command. You can shorten this to bind.
bind C-a send-prefix	Configures tmux to send the prefix when pressing the Prefix combination twice consecutively
bind -r [key] [command]	Creates a keybinding that is repeatable, meaning you only need to press the Prefix key once, and you can press the assigned key repeatedly afterward. This is useful for commands where you want to cycle through elements or resize panes. Can be shortened to bind
unbind-key [key]	Removes a defined keybinding so it can be bound to a different command. You can shorten this to unbind.
list-keys	Lists all keybindings, their associated commands, and any descriptions or notes
Prefix ?	Lists the default keybindings and their descriptions. Useful for unbinding default keys
display-message	Displays the given text in the status message. You can shorten this to display.
set -a	Appends values onto existing options rather than replacing the option's value
set -g mouse off	Disables mouse support in tmux. Set to on if you wish to use the mouse.

Command	Description
set -g default-terminal "tmux-256color"	Defines the terminal type for windows. Sets the value of TERM, which other programs will use. tmux-256color is recommended, but screen-256color ensures the widest compatibility with programs originally written for the screen program.

Commands to control tmux's appearance

Command	Description
set -g status-style	Sets the foreground and background color for the status line. Supports the options dim, bright (or bold), reverse, and blink in addition to colors
	Example: set -g status-style fg=white,bold,bg=black
set -w -g window-status-style	Sets the foreground and background color of the window list in the status line. Uses the same options as status-style
set -w -g window-status-current-style	Sets the foreground and background color of the active window in the window list in the status line. Uses the same options as status-style
set-w-gwindow-status-activity-style	Sets the foreground and background color of any window with background activity. Uses the same options as status-style
set -w -g pane-border-style	Sets the foreground and background color of the pane borders. Uses the same options as status-style
set -w -g pane-active-border-style	Sets the foreground and background color of the active pane's border. Uses the same options as status-style
set -w -g window-style	Sets the foreground and background color of the window. Uses the same options as status-style
set -w -g window-active-style	Sets the foreground and background color of the active window. Uses the same options as status-style
set -g message-style	Sets the foreground and background color of the message area and tmux command line. Uses the same options as status-style
set -g status-length-left and set -g status-length-right	Controls the number of visible characters in the left and right sides of the status line

Command	Description
set -g status-left and set -g status-right	Configures the items that appear in the left and right sides of the status line
set -g status-interval n	Defines the refresh interval for the status line, where n is the number of seconds between refreshes
set -g status-justify center	Centers the window list in the status line
set -w -g monitor-activity on	Looks for activity in other windows and highlights the name of the window with background activity
set -w -g visual-activity on	Displays a message in the message area when there is activity in another window

## CHAPTER 3

Scripting Customized tmux Environments

You probably run a wide collection of tools and programs as you work on your projects. If you're working on a full-stack web application, you most likely need to have a command shell, a database console, and another window dedicated to running your automated test suite for your application. If you use a shell-based editor like Vim or Emacs, you'll have that running, too. That's a lot of windows to manage and a lot of commands to type to get it all fired up.

Imagine being able to come to your workstation ready to tackle that new feature and being able to bring every one of those programs up, each in its own pane or window, in a single tmux session, using a single command. You can use tmux's client-server model to create custom scripts that build up your development environments, splitting windows and launching programs for you automatically. You'll do this manually first so that you gain a solid understanding of how tmux commands work. Then, you'll use a tool to automate this process.

Creating a Custom Setup with tmux Commands

You've already used the tmux command to create new sessions, but the tmux command takes many other options. You can use this command to target an existing session and split its windows into panes, change layouts, or even start up applications within the session.

The key to making this work is the -t switch, or the "target." When you have a named tmux session, you can attach to it like this:

```
$ tmux attach -t [session_name]
```

You use this target switch to direct a tmux command to the appropriate tmux session. Try it out.

Create a new tmux session called development, using the -s flag to specify the session name:

```
$ tmux new-session -s development
```

Then, detach from the session with Prefix d.

Even though you're no longer connected, you can split the window in the tmux session horizontally by issuing this command:

```
$ tmux split-window -h -t development
```

The split-window -h command should look familiar to you because you used this when you configured the | and - keys to split windows back on page 20. But this time, instead of binding it to a key, you're passing it to the tmux command and pointing it to a specific session.

When you attach to the session again, the window will split into two panes. Attach to your session again to see for yourself.

```
$ tmux attach -t development
```

You don't even have to detach from a tmux session to send commands to a running session. You can open another terminal and split the window again, but this time with a vertical split. Try it out. Open a second terminal window or tab and enter this command:

```
$ tmux split-window -v -t development
```

Using this approach, you can create customized environments for each of your projects. You'll explore this concept by creating your own development environment using a couple of approaches. You'll start by creating a script that issues various commands.

Scripting a Project Configuration

In Chapter 1, Learning the Basics, on page 1, you explored tmux commands such as new-session and new-window. You'll' use those commands and others to write a script that switches to your project directory, creates a new tmux session, and creates a window with a couple of panes and two additional windows with one pane each. To top it off, you'll launch applications in each of the panes.

Start by creating a new script called development in your home directory:

```
$ touch ~/development
```

Make this script executable so that you can run it like any other executable program from your shell:

```
$ chmod +x ~/development
```

When you run this script, you'll want it to change to the directory containing your project. For this example, use the directory devproject. But before you can change to that directory, you'd better create it first:

```
$ mkdir ~/devproject
```

Now, open the ~/development script in your text editor and add the following line to create a new tmux session called development:

scripting/development
```
tmux new-session -s development -n editor -d
```

You're passing a couple of additional parameters when you create this new session. First, you're creating this session and naming it with the -s flag like you've done before. Then, you give the initial window a name of editor and immediately detach from this new session with the -d flag.

Next, add a line to the script that uses tmux's send-keys command to change the current directory to the one you're using for the project:

```
tmux send-keys -t development 'cd ~/devproject' C-m
```

You place C-m at the end of the line to send the Carriage Return sequence, represented by Ctrl-M.[1] This is how you tell tmux to press the Enter key.

Use the same approach to open the Vim text editor in that window. Add this line to your script:

```
tmux send-keys -t development 'vim' C-m
```

With these three commands, you've created a new session, changed to a directory, and opened a text editor. But, your environment isn't yet complete. Split the main editor window so you have a small terminal window on the bottom for running quick shell commands. To do this, use the split-window command. Add this line to your script:

```
tmux split-window -v -t development
```

---

1. http://en.wikipedia.org/wiki/Carriage_return

This splits the main window in half horizontally. You could also specify a percentage like this:

```
tmux split-window -v -p 10 -t development
```

For this project, leave the split-window command as-is and then select one of the default tmux layouts—the main-horizontal one—by adding the following line to your script:

```
tmux select-layout -t development main-horizontal
```

You've created your window and split it into two panes, but the bottom pane needs to open in the project folder. You already know how to send commands to tmux instances, but now you have to target those commands at specific panes and windows.

Targeting Specific Panes and Windows

Commands such as send-keys let you specify the target window and pane in addition to the target session. In the configuration file you created back in Chapter 2, Configuring tmux, on page 15, you specified a base-index of 1, meaning that your window numbering starts at 1. This base index doesn't affect the panes, though, which is why you also set the pane-base-index to 1. In the project you're setting up, there are two panes arranged like this:

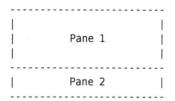

The Vim text editor is open in Pane 1, and its current working directory is set to the directory containing your project. Pane 2 has no applications running. You want to send a command to Pane 2 that changes the current working directory of that pane to the project directory so that both panes are using the same directory. You target a pane using the format [session]:[window].[pane], so to target Pane 2, you'd use development:1.2. So, add this line to your script, and you'll get exactly what you want:

```
tmux send-keys -t development:1.2 'cd ~/devproject' C-m
```

You now have a session with a text editor and a terminal, and the working directory in both panes is set. Next, you'll finish up this configuration by adding a couple more windows to the session.

Creating and Selecting Windows

Add a second window in the session that you can use as a full-screen console for running a local development server. Create that new window using the new-window command by adding the following lines to your script:

```
tmux new-window -n console -t development
tmux send-keys -t development:2 'cd ~/devproject' C-m
```

After you create the window, you use send-keys to once again change into the project directory. You only have one pane in the new window, so you only have to specify the window number in the target.

When you create a new window, tmux will switch to that window. When you start up your session, you probably want your first window with your text editor to be displayed instead. You do that with the select-window command. Add this to your script:

```
tmux select-window -t development:1
tmux attach -t development
```

You could continue to add to this script, creating additional windows and panes, starting up remote connections to your servers, tailing log files, connecting to database consoles, or even running commands that pull down the latest version of your code when you start working. But this is a good stopping point.

You've probably noticed that you've changed the working directory multiple times. The directory your tmux session starts in is the directory that all new windows and panes will use. You could modify the script so that it changes to the project directory before launching tmux, but that would change your current working directory outside of tmux as well. This script keeps things contained and illustrates a few options for the send-keys command.

End your script by finally attaching to the session so that it shows up on the screen, ready for you to begin working. The entire script looks like this:

```
tmux new-session -s development -n editor -d
tmux send-keys -t development 'cd ~/devproject' C-m
tmux send-keys -t development 'vim' C-m
tmux split-window -v -t development
tmux select-layout -t development main-horizontal
tmux send-keys -t development:1.2 'cd ~/devproject' C-m
tmux new-window -n console -t development
tmux send-keys -t development:2 'cd ~/devproject' C-m
tmux select-window -t development:1
tmux attach -t development
```

Run the script with the following command:

```
$ ~/development
```

Your environment will look like the following image:

One drawback to this approach is that this script creates a brand-new session each time, and it won't work properly if you run it a second time while the development session is currently running. To fix this, modify the script to check if a session with that name already exists by using the tmux has-session command and only create the session if it's not there:

scripting/reattach/development
```
if ! tmux has-session -t development
then
  tmux new-session -s development -n editor -d
  tmux send-keys -t development 'cd ~/devproject' C-m
  tmux send-keys -t development 'vim' C-m
  tmux split-window -v -t development
  tmux select-layout -t development main-horizontal
  tmux send-keys -t development:1.2 'cd ~/devproject' C-m
  tmux new-window -n console -t development
  tmux send-keys -t development:2 'cd ~/devproject' C-m
  tmux select-window -t development:1
fi
tmux attach -t development
```

This approach works well for a single project setup. You could modify this further by using a variable for the project name to make the script more generic, but you'll look at a couple of other ways you can configure things to manage multiple projects instead.

Using tmux Configuration Files for Setup

The .tmux.conf file itself can execute commands that set up a default environment. If you wanted every tmux session to start in the same default folder or automatically open a split window, you could bake that right into your default configuration by adding the appropriate commands to the end of your configuration file.

But you can also specify a configuration file when you start up an instance of tmux by using the -f flag. This way, you don't have to change your original default configuration file, and you can check your configuration file in with your project's source code. You can also set up your own per-project configuration options, such as new keyboard shortcuts to run commands or start your test suite.

Try it out. Create a new file called app.conf:

```
$ touch app.conf
```

Inside this file, you can use the same commands you explored in the previous section, but since you're inside the configuration file rather than a shell script, you don't have to explicitly prefix each command with tmux. Add this code to your app.conf file:

```
scripting/app.conf
source-file ~/.tmux.conf
new-session -s development -n editor -d
send-keys -t development 'cd ~/devproject' C-m
send-keys -t development 'vim' C-m
split-window -v -t development
select-layout -t development main-horizontal
send-keys -t development:1.2 'cd ~/devproject' C-m
new-window -n console -t development
send-keys -t development:2 'cd ~/devproject' C-m
select-window -t development:1
```

This code first loads your existing .tmux.conf file. This way, you'll have all the environment settings you previously defined, including your keybindings and status bar settings. This isn't mandatory, but if you left this off, you'd have to use all the default keybindings and options, or you'd have to redefine your options in this file. The rest of the commands perform the same actions as the previous script you wrote.

To use this configuration file, pass the -f flag followed by the path to the config file. You also have to start tmux with the attach command, like this:

```
$ tmux -f app.conf attach
```

This is because, by default, tmux always calls the new-session command when it starts. This file creates a new session already, so you'd have *two* tmux sessions running if you left off attach.

This approach gives you a lot of flexibility, but you can gain even more by using a command-line tool called tmuxinator.

Managing Configuration with tmuxinator

tmuxinator is a tool that lets you define and manage different tmux configurations. You define window layouts and commands in YAML format and then launch them with the tmuxinator command. Unlike the other approaches, tmuxinator offers a central location for your configurations and a much easier dialect for creating complex layouts. It also lets you specify commands that should always run before each window gets created.

tmuxinator requires the Ruby interpreter, so you'll need to have that on your system. If you're on a Mac, you already have Ruby installed. If you're on Linux or WSL, you can usually install Ruby through a package manager.

Install tmuxinator by using Rubygems, the package management system for Ruby:

```
$ sudo gem install tmuxinator
```

tmuxinator needs the $EDITOR shell environment to be defined, so if you haven't set yours yet, you'll want to do that in your shell configuration files. If you're using Bash, you'll use the ~/.bashrc file on Linux, or ~/.bash_profile on macOS. If you use zsh, you'll use ~/.zshrc.

For example, to define Vim as the default editor, you'd add this line to your shell configuration file:

```
export EDITOR=vim
```

Now, you can create a new tmuxinator project. Execute the following command to create a new project called development:

```
$ tmuxinator open development
```

This pops open the editor you assigned to the $EDITOR environment variable and displays the default project configuration, which looks like this:

scripting/default.yaml
```
# ~/.tmuxinator/development.yml

name: development
root: ~/
```

```
# a bunch of comments....
windows:
  - editor:
      layout: main-vertical
      # synchronize: after
      panes:
        - vim
        - guard
  - server: bundle exec rails s
  - logs: tail -f log/development.log
```

This default configuration creates a tmux session with three windows that works well for a Ruby on Rails project, which makes sense considering tmuxinator is written in Ruby. The first window is divided into two panes, using the main-vertical layout scheme. The left pane opens Vim, and the right pane opens Guard, a Ruby program that watches files for changes and executes tasks, like test runners. The second window launches Rails' built-in web server, and the third window uses the tail command to follow the application's development log file.

As you can see, tmuxinator makes it trivial to define not only the windows and panes but also what commands you want to execute in each one. To demonstrate this, you'll use tmuxinator to construct the same development environment you scripted by hand, with Vim in the top pane and a terminal on the bottom, starting in the ~/devproject folder. Remove the contents of this file and replace it with the following code:

scripting/development.yaml
```
name: development
root: ~/devproject
windows:
  - editor:
      layout: main-horizontal
      panes:
        - vim
        - #empty, will just run plain bash
  - console: # empty
```

The YAML file format uses two spaces for indenting, so it's really important to ensure you format the file correctly and that you don't accidentally use tabs when you write the file.

To fire up the new environment, save the config file and then execute the following command:

```
$ tmuxinator development
```

tmuxinator automatically loads up your original *.tmux.conf* file, applies the settings, and then arranges the windows and panes for you, just like you specified. If you want to make more changes to your environment, execute the tmuxinator open again:

```
$ tmuxinator open development
```

Your shell editor will open, and you can make additional changes. Once you save those changes, you will need to close the tmux session completely to apply them.

By default, the configuration files for tmuxinator are located in *~/.config/tmuxinator/*, so you can find those and back them up or share them with others.

Under the hood, tmuxinator is constructing a script that executes the individual tmux commands just like you did when you wrote your own script. However, it's a nicer syntax that's easy to follow. It does require a Ruby interpreter on your machine, though, so it may not be something you'll set up on every environment where you'd like to use tmux. However, you can use tmuxinator to generate a configuration you can use anywhere. The tmuxinator debug command displays the script that tmuxinator will use:

```
$ tmuxinator debug development
```

Here's what the output looks like, with unnecessary comments removed for brevity:

```bash
#!/bin/bash
unset RBENV_VERSION
unset RBENV_DIR

tmux start-server;

cd /home/brian/devproject

  TMUX= tmux new-session -d -s development -n editor
  tmux send-keys -t development:1 cd\ /home/brian/devproject C-m

  tmux new-window -c /home/brian/devproject -t development:2 -n console
  # Window "editor"
  tmux send-keys -t development:1.1 vim C-m

  tmux splitw -c /home/brian/devproject -t development:1
  tmux select-layout -t development:1 tiled
  tmux select-layout -t development:1 tiled
  tmux select-layout -t development:1 main-horizontal
  tmux select-pane -t development:1.1

  # Window "console"

  tmux select-window -t development:1
```

```
tmux select-pane -t development:1.1

if [ -z "$TMUX" ]; then
  tmux -u attach-session -t development
else
  tmux -u switch-client -t development
fi
```

You could save the output of tmuxinator debug to a script you can run on any machine. You can also use this option to troubleshoot any issues you might be having as you develop your configuration file or use this as the basis for your own script, which you then further customize.

What's Next?

You can use every tmux command through the shell, which means you can write scripts to automate nearly every aspect of tmux, including running sessions. For example, you could create a keybinding in tmux that sources a shell script that divides the current window into two panes and logs you into your production web and database servers.

You've done a lot so far. You know how to set up projects, move around panes and windows, and launch various programs within tmux. You've tinkered around with your configuration enough to understand how to customize things to your liking. And you've experimented with three separate ways to script out your tmux environment. But, as you start to integrate tmux into your workflow, you'll start to notice some new challenges crop up. For example, the results of tests or application logs start to scroll off the screen, and you'll want to be able to scroll up to read things. Also, you'll want to copy and paste text between panes, windows, or other applications. So, next, you'll work with tmux's output buffers.

For Future Reference

Scriptable tmux commands

Command	Description
tmux new-session -s development -n editor	Creates a session named development and names the first window editor
tmux attach -t development	Attaches to a session named development
tmux send-keys -t development '[keys]' C-m	Sends the keystrokes to the development session's active window or pane. C-m is equivalent to pressing the Enter key.

Command	Description
tmux send-keys -t development:1.1 '[keys]' C-m	Sends the keystrokes to the development session's first window and first pane, provided the window and pane indexes are set to 1. C-m is equivalent to pressing the Enter key.
tmux select-window -t development:1	Selects the first window of development, making it the active window
tmux split-window -v -p 10 -t development	Splits the current window in the development session vertically, dividing it in half *horizontally*, and sets its height to 10% of the total window size
tmux select-layout -t development main-horizontal	Sets the layout for the development session to main-horizontal
tmux source-file [file]	Loads the specified tmux configuration file
tmux -f app.conf attach	Loads the app.conf configuration file and attaches to a session created within the app.conf file

tmuxinator commands

Command	Description
tmuxinator open [name]	Opens the configuration file for the project name in the default text editor. Creates the configuration if it doesn't exist
tmuxinator [name]	Loads the tmux session for the given project. Creates the session from the contents of the project's configuration file if no session currently exists, or attaches to the session
tmuxinator list	Lists all current projects
tmuxinator copy [source] [destination]	Copies a project configuration
tmuxinator delete [name]	Deletes the specified project
tmuxinator implode	Deletes all current projects
tmuxinator doctor	Looks for problems with the tmuxinator and system configuration
tmuxinator debug	Shows the script that tmuxinator will run, helping you figure out what's going wrong

## CHAPTER 4

Working With Text and Buffers

Throughout the course of your average day, you'll copy and paste text more times than you can keep track of. When you're working with tmux, you'll eventually come to the point where you need to scroll backward through the terminal's output buffer to see something that scrolled off the screen. You might also need to copy some text and paste it into a file or into another program. This chapter is all about how to manage the text inside your sessions. You'll see how to use the keyboard to scroll through tmux's output buffer, how to work with multiple paste buffers, and how to work with the system clipboard.

Scrolling Through Output with Copy Mode

When you work with programs in the terminal, it's common that the output from these programs scrolls off the screen. But when you use tmux, you can use the keyboard to move backward through the output buffer so that you can see what you missed. This is especially useful for those times when you're running tests or watching log files, and you can't just rely on the less command or your text editor.

Pressing `Prefix` `[` places you in Copy mode. You can then use your movement keys to move the cursor around the screen. By default, the arrow keys work. But in Chapter 2, Configuring tmux, on page 15, you configured tmux to use Vim keys for moving between windows and resizing panes so you wouldn't have to take your hands off the home row. tmux has a vi mode for working with the buffer as well. To enable it, add this line to .tmux.conf:

buffers/tmux.conf
```
# Enable vi keys.
set -w -g mode-keys vi
```

With this option set, you can use `h`, `j`, `k`, and `l` to move around your buffer.

To get out of Copy mode, press the `Enter` key. Moving around one character at a time isn't very efficient. Since you enabled vi mode, you can also use some other visible shortcuts to move around the buffer.

For example, you can use `w` to jump to the next word and `b` to jump back one word. And you can use `f`, followed by any character, to jump to that character on the same line and `F` to jump backward on the line.

Moving Quickly Through the Buffer

When you have several pages of buffered output, moving the cursor around to scroll isn't going to be that useful. Instead of moving word by word or character by character, you can scroll through the buffer page by page or jump to the beginning or end of the buffer.

You can move up one page with `Ctrl`-`b` and down one page with `Ctrl`-`f`. You can jump all the way to the top of the buffer's history with `g` and then jump all the way to the bottom with `G`.

Searching Through the Buffer

You don't have to browse through the hundreds of lines of content page by page if you know what you're looking for. By pressing `?` in Copy mode, you can search upwards for phrases or keywords. Simply press `?`, type in the search phrase, and press `Enter` to jump to the first occurrence of the phrase. Then press `n` to jump to the next occurrence, or `N` to move to the previous.

To search downward, press `/` instead of `?`. Pressing `n` then jumps to the next occurrence, and `N` jumps to the previous occurrence.

Getting comfortable moving around the buffer this way will dramatically speed you up. It's faster to type the word you want to move to instead of using the arrows to move around, especially if you're looking through the output of log files.

Now, let's explore how to copy text from one pane and paste it into another. This is Copy mode, after all.

Copying and Pasting Text

Moving around and looking for things in the output buffer is usually only half the equation. You often need to copy some text so you can do something useful with it. tmux's Copy mode gives us the opportunity to select and copy text to a paste buffer so you can dump that text elsewhere.

To copy text, enter Copy mode and move the cursor to where you want to start selecting text. Then press Space and move the cursor to the end of the text. When you press Enter, the selected text gets copied into a paste buffer.

To paste the contents you just captured, press Prefix].

Let's look at a few ways to copy and paste text from the main output buffer.

Capturing a Pane

tmux has a handy shortcut that copies the entire visible contents of a pane to a paste buffer. Enter tmux's Command mode with Prefix : and type the following command:

capture-pane

The contents of the pane will be in a paste buffer. You can then paste that content into another pane or window by pressing Prefix].

When you capture a pane, tmux captures the text exactly as it's displayed. If the pane's width is too small, causing text to wrap to the next line, tmux will preserve the line break when you capture the pane by inserting newline characters into the captured text. To avoid this, pass the -J option to capture-pane. The copied text will no longer contain newline characters.

Showing, Saving, and Loading the Buffer

You can display the contents of your paste buffer by using the show-buffer command in Command mode or from a terminal session like this:

```
$ tmux show-buffer
```

By using the save-buffer command, you can save the buffer to a file, which can often be a real time saver.

You can capture the contents of the current pane to a text file. In Command mode, execute the command capture-pane; save-buffer buffer.txt to capture the pane and save it to the file buffer.txt. You could easily map that command to a keystroke if you wanted.

Finally, you can load a file into the buffer with load-buffer. In Command Mode, execute the command load-buffer buffer.txt to load buffer.txt back into the buffer.

Using Multiple Paste Buffers

tmux maintains a stack of paste buffers, which means you can copy text without replacing the buffer's existing content. This is much more flexible than the traditional clipboard offered by the operating system.

Every time you copy some new text, tmux creates a new paste buffer, putting the new buffer at the top of the stack. To demonstrate, fire up a new tmux session and load up a text editor such as Vim or Nano within the session. In the editor, type the following sentences, one per line:

```
First sentence is first.
Next sentence is next.
Last sentence is last.
```

Now copy some text to the paste buffer using tmux. Enter Copy mode with Prefix [. Move to the start of the first sentence, press Space to start selecting text, move to the end of the first sentence, and press Enter to copy the selection. Repeat this with the second and third sentences.

Each time you copy text, tmux creates a new buffer. You can see these buffers with the list-buffers command. Issue that command through Command mode in tmux and you'll see three buffers, each containing one of the lines you copied:

```
buffer2: 22 bytes: "Last sentence is last."
buffer1: 22 bytes: "Next sentence is next."
buffer0: 25 bytes: "First sentence is first."
```

Pressing Prefix] always pastes the most recently captured text, but you can issue the command choose-buffer to select a buffer and paste the contents into the focused pane.

Split the current window in half and launch Nano in the second pane, then enter Command mode and type this:

choose-buffer

You'll be presented with a list that looks like this:

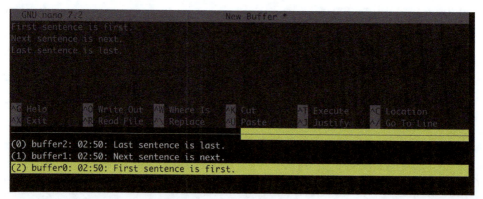

You can select any entry in the list, press Enter , and the text will be inserted into the selected pane automatically.

This is an excellent way to manage multiple bits of text, especially in text-based environments where you don't have access to an OS-level clipboard.

These buffers are shared across *all* running tmux sessions, too, so you can take content from one session and paste it into another.

Notice that each buffer has a name when you run the list-buffers command:

```
buffer2: 22 bytes: "Last sentence is last."
buffer1: 22 bytes: "Next sentence is next."
buffer0: 25 bytes: "First sentence is first."
```

The paste-buffer command lets you specify the source. Instead of pressing Prefix -] to paste the most recently copied text, enter Command Mode and use paste-buffer and specify the buffer you want to paste from. For example, to grab the text from buffer1, enter the following command in Command Mode:

```
paste-buffer -b buffer1
```

If you don't like these default buffer names, you can rename a buffer. Enter Command Mode and issue the following command to change buffer2 to something easier to remember:

```
set-buffer -b buffer2 -n last-sentence
```

Now, when you look at the list of buffers, you'll see the buffer's name has changed:

```
➤ last-sentence: 22 bytes: "Last sentence is last."
  buffer1: 22 bytes: "Next sentence is next."
  buffer0: 25 bytes: "First sentence is first."
```

There is no direct way to use save-buffer to copy text into a buffer and specify the name at the same time. However, you can do this with a custom keybinding. You will see an example of that in Integrating tmux with System Clipboards, on page 58. However, the load-buffer command lets you load text into a named buffer if you pass the -b flag. For example, to load the contents of buffer.txt into a buffer called code, enter Command Mode and use load-buffer -b code buffer.txt.

Remapping Copy and Paste Keys

If you use Vim and you'd like to make the copy and paste command keys a little more familiar, you can remap the keys in your configuration. For example, you can use Prefix Escape to enter Copy mode, then use v to start Visual mode to select your text, use y to "yank" text into the buffer, and use p to paste the text:

```
buffers/tmux.conf
bind Escape copy-mode
bind -T copy-mode-vi v send -X begin-selection
bind -T copy-mode-vi y send -X copy-selection
unbind p
bind p paste-buffer
```

This can be a real productivity boost if you happen to do a lot of copying and pasting between windows and panes and are already comfortable with the keys that Vim uses.

Now that you understand how buffers work, and how to change keys related to copying and pasting text, you can integrate tmux with your operating system's clipboard.

Integrating tmux with System Clipboards

As you integrate tmux into your development workflow, you'll find that you'll have to work with text from other programs. When you copy text in tmux, it ends up in its own buffers, separate from your system clipboard that other applications can access. But with some helper apps and some custom keybindings, you can share the system clipboard with tmux.

Working with the Clipboard on Linux

You can integrate your buffers with the Linux system clipboard so you can more easily copy and paste between programs. The method you use depends on whether or not your distribution uses Xorg or Wayland for the display system.

If your system uses Xorg, you'll need the xclip utility,[1] On Ubuntu, use the apt command to install the xclip package:

```
$ sudo apt install xclip
```

If your system uses Wayland, you'll use wl-copy and wl-paste from the wl-clipboard package. Install this package on Ubuntu with:

```
$ sudo apt install wl-clipboard
```

Now you can add keybindings that use tmux's save-buffer and set-buffer commands with the system clipboard.

First, add the following lines to detect the display manager and set the copy and paste commands to variables:

---

1. http://sourceforge.net/projects/xclip/

buffers/linux/tmux.conf
```
# Detect the display server protocol and set clipboard commands
if-shell '[ "$XDG_SESSION_TYPE" = "wayland" ]' \
    'set -g copy-command "wl-copy"; \
    set -g paste-command "wl-paste -n"' \
    'set -g copy-command "xclip -sel clip -i"; \
    set -g paste-command "xclip -sel clip -o"'
```

To copy the current buffer to the system clipboard, add this command to the .tmux.conf file:

buffers/linux/tmux.conf
```
# Prefix Ctrl-C takes what's in the buffer and sends it to system clipboard
# via the command stored in the variable.
bind C-c run 'tmux save-buffer - | $copy_command'
```

This configures Prefix Ctrl - c so it pipes the current buffer to xclip or wl-copy. The hyphen after save-buffer instructs tmux to use standard output rather than a file.

To use this keybinding, enter Copy mode with Prefix - [, select your text, press y , and then press Prefix Ctrl - c to get your text on the clipboard. You can speed up the process by binding the y key to send the output to the system clipboard directly:

buffers/linux/tmux.conf
```
# y in copy mode takes selection and sends it to system clipboard via the
# command stored in the variable.
bind -T copy-mode-vi y send-keys -X copy-pipe-and-cancel '$copy_command'
```

Now, the text you select and copy in Copy mode will be on your system clipboard.

To paste text from the system clipboard into a tmux session, add the following line to your configuration:

buffers/linux/tmux.conf
```
# Prefix Ctrl-v fills tmux buffer from system clipboard, then
# pastes from buffer into tmux window
bind C-v run-shell '$paste_command | tmux load-buffer - \; paste-buffer'
```

This configures tmux to pull the content from xclip or wl-paste into a new tmux buffer and then paste it into the selected tmux window or pane when you press Prefix Ctrl - v .

Using macOS Clipboard Commands

If you are a Mac user, you may be familiar with macOS's command-line clipboard utilities pbcopy and pbpaste. These utilities make it a snap to work with the clipboard. The pbcopy command captures text to the system clipboard, and the pbpaste command pastes content out. For example, you can use pbcopy and cat together to easily put the contents of your .tmux.conf file into the clipboard so you can paste it in an email or on the web, like this:

```
$ cat ~/.tmux.conf | pbcopy
```

You can use pbcopy inside of tmux as well. For example, you can send the contents of the current tmux buffer to the system clipboard:

```
$ tmux save-buffer - | pbcopy
```

Or, you can paste the clipboard contents into tmux:

```
$ tmux set-buffer $(pbpaste); tmux paste-buffer
```

This means that you can also create keyboard shortcuts to do this, just like you did in Working with the Clipboard on Linux, on page 58. Add the following code to your configuration:

```
buffers/mac/tmux.conf
# Prefix Ctrl-C takes what's in the buffer and sends it to system clipboard
# via pbcopy
bind C-c run "tmux save-buffer - | pbcopy"
```

To use this, first select some text and copy it to tmux's buffer. Then, press Prefix Ctrl - c to copy it to the system clipboard.

That's a lot of steps. Just like with Linux, you can configure tmux's Copy mode to send the text you copy directly to the system clipboard by adding this keybinding to your configuration:

```
buffers/mac/tmux.conf
# y in copy mode takes selection and sends it to system clipboard via pbcopy
bind -T copy-mode-vi y send-keys -X copy-pipe-and-cancel "pbcopy"
```

Now, when you select text in Copy mode and press y, the text will be sent to pbcopy and will be on your system clipboard, ready for use in other programs.

To support pasting from the system clipboard, add this longer command, which fills the buffer with the system clipboard contents and then pastes the buffer into the tmux window:

```
buffers/mac/tmux.conf
# Prefix Ctrl-v fills tmux buffer from system clipboard via pbpaste, then
# pastes from buffer into tmux window
bind C-v run "tmux set-buffer \"$(pbpaste)\"; tmux paste-buffer"
```

This makes the process of copying and pasting code much easier.

What's Next?

By using tmux paste buffers to move text around, you gain the ability to have a clipboard in situations where you might not have one, such as when you're logged into the console of a server or without a graphical terminal. Being able to scroll back through the history of a long console output can be a huge help. It's worth installing tmux directly on your servers for that reason alone.

Now that you have a good understanding of how to find, copy, and paste text, you can start working tmux into your daily routine. For many developers, pair programming is often part of that routine. In the next chapter, you'll discover how to use tmux to work with another developer.

For Future Reference

Shortcut keys

Shortcut	Description
`Prefix` `[`	Enters Copy mode
`Prefix` `]`	Pastes current buffer contents
`Prefix` `=`	Lists all paste buffers and pastes selected buffer contents

Copy mode movement keys (vi mode)

Command	Description
`h`, `j`, `k`, and `l`	Moves the cursor left, down, up, and right, respectively
`w`	Moves the cursor forward one word at a time
`b`	Moves the cursor backward one word at a time
`f` followed by any character	Moves to the next occurrence of the specified character
`F` followed by any character	Moves to the previous occurrence of the specified character
`Ctrl`-`b`	Scrolls up one page
`Ctrl`-`f`	Scrolls down one page
`g`	Jumps to the top of the buffer
`G`	Jumps to the bottom of the buffer
`?`	Starts a search backward through the buffer
`/`	Starts a search forward through the buffer

Commands

Command	Description
show-buffer	Displays current buffer contents
capture-pane	Captures the selected pane's visible contents to a new buffer
save-buffer [filename]	Saves the buffer's contents to the specified file
load-buffer [filename]	Loads the file's contents into the buffer
load-buffer -b buffername [filename]	Loads the file's contents into the buffer with the specified name
list-buffers	Lists all paste buffers
choose-buffer	Shows paste buffers and pastes the contents of the one you select
set-buffer -b buffer2 -n last-sentence	Renames buffer2 to last-sentence
paste-buffer -b buffer1	Pastes the contents of buffer1 into the selected pane

## CHAPTER 5

Pair Programming with tmux

Up until now, you've been making configuration changes and learning how to work within tmux on your own machine. But, one of the most popular uses of tmux by developers is pair programming. It was actually my first introduction to tmux, and I immediately saw the potential as my friend walked me through using its various features.

Pair programming has many benefits. Working with another developer can help you see things you might not have seen on your own, but unless you're physically in the same location, pair programming can be somewhat difficult. Screen sharing through Google Meet, Zoom, or other tools takes up a lot of bandwidth and can be dodgy when you're not using the best network connection. In this chapter, you'll configure and use tmux for pair programming so that you can work remotely with another developer on even the slowest hotel Wi-Fi connection.

There are two ways to work with remote users. The first method involves creating a new user account that you and others share. You set up tmux and your development environment under that account and use it as a shared workspace. The second approach uses tmux's sockets, where you can have a second user connect to your tmux session without having to share your user account.

Both methods have an inherent security flaw: they let someone else see things on your screen and in your account. You're inviting someone in to potentially look at your files. To get around this, it's wise to use an intermediate server for pairing. Using a low-cost cloud instance or virtual machine with VirtualBox[1] and Vagrant,[2] you can quickly create a development environment for pairing.

---

1. https://www.virtualbox.org/
2. https://www.vagrantup.com/docs/getting-started/

In this chapter, you'll be working with a remote server as we explore both of these approaches.

Pairing with a Shared Account

Using a shared account is the quickest way to work with another user. In a nutshell, you enable SSH access on the machine that will act as the host, install and configure tmux on that machine, and create a tmux session there. The second user logs into that machine with the same user account and attaches to the session. By using SSH public keys, you can make the login process somewhat transparent. Let's walk through the setup. For this example, you'll use a server called puzzles running Ubuntu that has the SSH daemon installed.

First, log in to the server with an account that has the ability to create additional accounts.

Once logged in, create a tmux user on the server. This is the user account everyone will use to connect to the pairing session. On the remote server, execute the following command:

```
brian@puzzles$ sudo adduser tmux
```

You want to configure the account so you can take SSH keys from other developers and use them to log into this account. You do this by creating the file ~/.ssh/authorized_keys under the tmux account. So, use the su command to switch to the user:

```
brian@puzzles$ sudo su - tmux
```

Then, create the .ssh folder and the .ssh/authorized_keys file, setting the appropriate permissions. Only the tmux user should be allowed to read, write, or execute the folder and file.

```
tmux@puzzles$ mkdir ~/.ssh
tmux@puzzles$ touch ~/.ssh/authorized_keys
tmux@puzzles$ chmod 700 ~/.ssh
tmux@puzzles$ chmod 600 ~/.ssh/authorized_keys
```

Each user you'd like to connect needs a public key, which they would generate on their local machine. To generate a key, use the ssh-keygen command:

```
$ ssh-keygen
```

Follow the prompts on the screen. Adding a passphrase is optional but does add an extra layer of security.

You then transfer the public keys to the server by adding them to the authorized_keys file. There are a number of ways to do this, but the most universal approach is to use cat and ssh to transfer the key and append it to authorized_keys at the same time, like this:

```
$ cat ~/.ssh/id_rsa.pub | ssh tmux@puzzles 'cat >> .ssh/authorized_keys'
```

Note that the second cat command uses >>, which appends to a file, whereas a single > would overwrite the file. Double-check your commands.

You'll be prompted for the tmux user's password before you can connect.

The command ssh-copy-id makes this process slightly easier. If you install this command using your package manager on your client, then you can transfer the key like this:

```
$ ssh-copy-id tmux@your_server
```

This command copies the .id_rsa.pub file and automatically appends it to .authorized_keys.

You can repeat this process for other users you want to share this account with.

If the person you want to pair with has a GitHub account, you can often obtain their SSH public key by visiting their GitHub profile and appending .keys to the end of the URL. For example, to see the public keys for the user myusername, visit https://github.com/myusername.keys. You can then copy the key or keys from the results and paste them into the .authorized_keys file.

With the keys in place, you can install tmux, text editors, compilers, programming languages, and version control systems. You can then log into the tmux account and configure tmux and your environment just like you would on any other development environment.

You create a new named tmux session on the server. Run the following command to create a session called Pairing:

```
tmux@puzzles$ tmux new-session -s Pairing
```

Another member of your team can log in to the same machine and attach to the session with the following command:

```
tmux@puzzles$ tmux attach -t Pairing
```

You can then work collaboratively on the project. What's more, you can detach from the session and reattach to it later, which means you can leave your environment running for days or even weeks at a time. You'd have a persistent development environment you can log into from anywhere that has a terminal with SSH support.

Using a Shared Account and Grouped Sessions

When two people are attached to the same tmux session, they usually both see the same thing and interact with the same windows. But there are times when it's helpful if one person can work in a different window without completely taking over control.

Using "grouped sessions," you can do just that. Test this out by creating a new session on your remote server called groupedsession:

```
tmux@puzzles$ tmux new-session -s groupedsession
```

Then, instead of attaching to the session, another user can join that session by *creating a new session* by specifying the target of the original session groupedsession and then specifying their *own* session name, like this:

```
tmux@puzzles$ tmux new-session -t groupedsession -s mysession
```

When the second session launches, both users can interact with the session at the same time, just as if the second user had attached to the session. However, each user can create windows independently of the other. So, if your new user creates a window, you'll both see the new window show up in the status line, but you'll stay on the window you're currently working in. This is great for those "hey, let me just try something" moments or when one person wants to use Emacs and the other person prefers Vim:

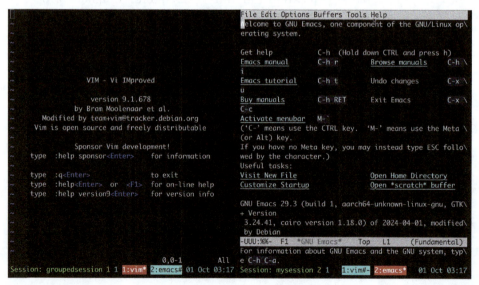

The second user can kill off their session with kill-session, and the original will still exist. However, both sessions will be killed if all windows are closed, so be careful.

That's a lot of work to go through if you just want someone to jump in and help you out with some code. So, let's look at a simple alternative that takes almost no time to set up.

Quickly Pairing with Upterm

Upterm[3] is a command-line tool designed to make pair programming with tmux painless. Using Upterm, you can quickly invite another developer to collaborate. When you launch Upterm, it generates an address that your pair can use to make the connection. Upterm's servers handle tunneling the connection for you. Let's look at how to use it.

First, ensure that you have an SSH key generated for your user. Upterm requires it to connect securely to other computers. Then install Upterm.

On macOS, you can install it with Homebrew:

```
$ brew install owenthereal/upterm/upterm
```

On other systems, you can grab the binary from the Releases page on GitHub[4] and copy the file to a place on your system PATH.

Once Upterm is installed, you can use it to share your terminal session with others. Upterm expects you to specify the command you want to share. You can also force a command to fire when a client connects. To share a tmux session called pairing with Upterm and have clients automatically join the session, use the following command:

```
$ upterm host --force-command 'tmux attach -t pairing' \
  -- tmux new -t pairing
```

The --force-command flag executes when the client connects, joining them to the session.

When Upterm launches, it displays details about the host:

```
=== Q3HGXYSAUDDSRJJXBDCM
Command:              tmux new -t pairing
Force Command:        tmux attach -t pairing
Host:                 ssh://uptermd.upterm.dev:22
SSH Session:          ssh Q3H...@uptermd.upterm.dev
```

---

3. https://upterm.dev/
4. https://github.com/owenthereal/upterm/releases

```
Run 'upterm session current' to display this screen again
Press <q> or <ctrl-c> to accept connections...
```

Copy the SSH Session command and send it to your pair, and they'll be able to join you instantly. You can test this out yourself by opening another terminal window and pasting the command into the second window.

Upterm won't allow any connections until you dismiss the message with q or Ctrl + c .

Once inside the session, you can see the session connection information again by executing the following command:

```
$ upterm session current
```

When you exit your tmux session, the external connection will be disconnected as well.

When you use Upterm, it lets the person on the other end of the connection type with you and potentially access all of your files. You can start Upterm in "read-only" mode if you need to demonstrate something and don't want anyone else to be able to type. Run upterm host with the -r flag:

```
$ upterm host -r --force-command 'tmux attach -t pairing' \
  -- tmux new -t pairing
```

Using Upterm with Your Own Servers

If you feel uncomfortable going through uptermd.upterm.dev to connect to other sessions, you can find instructions for setting up your own server at the Upterm website.[a] It provides you with the server, which you compile and install on your own Linux server. Then, you run the server and configure client machines to use that server instead of the default service. This may add more security, but you'll want to think about redundancy and availability. For example, the upterm.dev address resolves to multiple backend servers, ensuring high availability. If you want to ensure continuity, you'll want to configure your environment in a similar way.

---

a.   https://upterm.dev/

Using shared accounts or Upterm is easy, but it's not always desirable to share user accounts with team members or let someone remotely access your development machine. Let's look at an alternative approach.

Pairing with Separate Accounts and Sockets

Sharing accounts might not be the best approach. When you share an account, you are stuck using a shared home directory, which might lack the customizations you'd want. Using tmux's support for sockets, you can create sessions that multiple users can connect to with ease. This way, each user has their own home directory and set of files, but they can still collaborate through a shared tmux session.

To test this out, create two new user accounts for the session: one called ted and another named barney:

```
tmux@puzzles$ sudo adduser ted
```

```
tmux@puzzles$ sudo adduser barney
```

Next, create a tmux group and a /var/tmux folder that will hold the shared sessions.

```
tmux@puzzles$ sudo addgroup tmux
```

```
tmux@puzzles$ sudo mkdir /var/tmux
```

Change the group ownership of the /var/tmux folder so that the tmux group has access:

```
tmux@puzzles$ sudo chgrp tmux /var/tmux
```

Then, alter the permissions on the folder so that new files will be accessible for all members of the tmux group:

```
tmux@puzzles$ sudo chmod g+ws /var/tmux
```

Finally, add ted and barney to the tmux group:

```
tmux@puzzles$ sudo usermod -aG tmux ted
```

```
tmux@puzzles$ sudo usermod -aG tmux barney
```

Now, let's look at how these users can work together on a project.

Creating and Sharing Sessions

So far, you've used the new-session command to create these sessions, but that uses the default socket location, which won't be reachable by every user. You can create tmux sessions using the -S switch, which lets you specify a socket file.

Log in to your remote server as ted and create a new tmux session using a socket file in the /var/tmux/ folder you created:

```
ted@puzzles$ tmux -S /var/tmux/pairing new -s sharedsession
```

In that tmux session, give the barney user read and write access to the /var/tmux/pairing socket:

```
ted@puzzles$ chmod g+rw /var/tmp/tmux-share/pairing
```

Adding access to the socket isn't enough. You have to tell tmux that barney can have access to the tmux server. Execute this command:

```
ted@puzzles$ tmux server-access -a barney
```

You can make the access read-only by adding the -r flag:

```
ted@puzzles$ tmux server-access -a -r barney
```

In another terminal window, log in as barney and then attach to the session. But instead of specifying the target with the -t switch, specify the location of the socket file, like this:

```
barney@puzzles$ tmux -S /var/tmux/pairing attach
```

The barney user now attaches to the tmux session and sees everything that the ted user sees.

It's important to note that when using this approach, the .tmux.conf file used is the one that started up the session. Having two separate accounts doesn't mean that each account gets to use their own configuration files within the tmux session, but it does mean they can customize their accounts for other purposes, and can each initiate their own tmux session as needed. More importantly, it keeps barney out of ted's home directory. Also, since this is a shared session, the session will end when either person ends the session.

What's Next?

Now that you know how to use tmux to share your screen with others, you can use it for remote training, impromptu collaboration on open-source projects, or even presentations.

In addition, you can use this technique to fire up a tmux session on one of your production servers, load up monitoring tools or consoles, and then detach from it, leaving those tools running in the background. Then, you connect to your server, reattach to the session, and everything is back where you left it. I do something similar with one of my development environments. I set up tmux on a low-cost cloud server which lets me use nothing more than an iPad, an SSH client, and a Bluetooth keyboard to hack on code when I'm away from home. It even works brilliantly over slow networks.

Pair programming and working remotely are just two examples of how incorporating tmux into your workflow can make you more productive. In the next chapter, you'll look at other enhancements you can make to your environment as you explore advanced ways to work with windows, panes, and your system in general.

For Future Reference

Command	Description
tmux new-session -t [existing session] -s [new session]	Creates a connection to a grouped session
tmux show-messages	Displays a log of messages in the current window, useful for debugging
tmux -S [socket]	Creates a new session using a socket instead of a name
tmux -S [socket] attach	Attaches to an existing session using a socket instead of a name

## CHAPTER 6

Workflows

tmux is more than just a way to interact with your terminal sessions. You can use it to accelerate your work. In this chapter, you will explore some common and uncommon configurations and commands that you may find useful in your day-to-day work. You'll try some advanced ways to manage your panes and sessions, make tmux work with your shell of choice, extend tmux commands with external scripts, create keybindings that execute several commands, hook into tmux's processes, make popup menus, and look at tmux plugins. Let's start with windows and panes.

Working Effectively with Panes and Windows

Throughout this book, you've seen ways to divide up your tmux sessions into panes and windows. Once you've divided them, you may want to work with them in different ways depending on your situation.

Turning a Pane into a Window

Panes are great for dividing up a workspace so you can see multiple programs at once, but sometimes, you might want to "pop out" a pane into its own window. tmux has a command to do just that.

Inside any pane, press `Prefix` `!` and tmux will create a new window from your pane, removing the original pane. The new window is focused and appears in the tmux status bar. Use `Prefix` `p` to return to the previous window. You may also want to rename this window, which you can do with `Prefix` `,` (a comma).

Turning a Window into a Pane

If you have too many windows or you've created a new window from a pane, you may want to consolidate things. You can take a window and turn it into a pane with the join-pane command.

Try it out. Create a new tmux session with three windows:

```
$ tmux new-session -s panes -n first -d
$ tmux new-window -t panes -n second
$ tmux new-window -t panes -n third
$ tmux attach -t panes
```

When you attach to the session, you'll be in the third window. To move the first window into a pane in the current window, press Prefix : to enter Command mode, and type the following command:

join-pane -s panes:1

This means "Take window 1 of the panes session and join it to the current window." With the join-pane command, you specify the source window and pane, followed by the target window and pane. If you leave the target off, the currently focused window becomes the target. And if a window only has one pane, you can skip specifying the pane. Remember that you set the window and pane base indexes to 1 instead of 0 back in Chapter 2, Configuring tmux, on page 15. If you didn't do that, you'll have to use 0 instead.

You can also use this technique to move panes around. Your first window is gone since you joined it to the third window. You're left with two windows now. To move the second pane of the second window to the first, type this command:

join-pane -s panes:2.2 -t panes:1

Now, the first window has two panes and the second pane only has one.

When you "join" a pane, you're essentially moving a pane from one session to another. That means you can specify a different source session, using the notation [session_name]:[window].[pane], and you can specify a target window using the -t flag using the same notation. This lets you pull panes from one session into another. For example, if you had a tmux session called development, you could move a pane from the panes session to the development session:

join-pane -s panes:1.1 -t development:2

This command would move the first pane of the first window in the panes session to the first window of the development session. As you work with multiple tmux sessions, you'll appreciate the ability to move things around like this.

Maximizing and Restoring Panes

Sometimes, you want a pane to go full-screen for a bit so you can see its contents or work in a more focused way. You could use the break-pane command to move the pane to its own window but then you'd have to use join-pane to put it back where it was. Thankfully, tmux's developers recognized this need and built it in.

The resize-pane command accepts the -Z option for zooming a pane. Best of all, it's already mapped to `Prefix` `z`, and pressing it again restores the pane to its original size.

Launching Commands in Panes

In Chapter 3, Scripting Customized tmux Environments, on page 41, you used shell commands and send-keys to launch programs in your panes, but you can also execute commands automatically when you launch a window or a pane. When you create a new session or split a window, you can pass the command you want to execute as the last argument.

Let's use an example. You have two servers, burns and smithers, which run your web server and database server, respectively. When you start up tmux, you want to connect to both of these servers using a single window with two panes. The following commands do just that:

```
$ tmux new-session -s servers -d "ssh deploy@burns"
$ tmux split-window -t servers -v "ssh dba@smithers"
$ tmux attach -t servers
```

The first command creates the new session and connects to the burns server and detaches from the session. The second command divides the window into two panes using a vertical split and then connects to the smithers server. The last command attaches to the session.

When you issue commands this way, the window or pane closes when the command completes. In this example, when you log off of your remote servers, the pane or window will close.

You can use this method to launch programs in a split and have them close when the program finishes. It's great for builds or test runners, especially if you create a custom keybinding that launches these commands.

For example, you can define a key binding that maps `Prefix` `R` to open up the Node.js console:

```
bind-key R run "(tmux split-window -v node)"
```

Once you've defined this and reloaded your tmux configuration, pressing `Prefix` `R` splits the current pane in half and loads the Node.js REPL on the bottom. When you close the REPL with `Ctrl`+`d`, the pane automatically closes.

If you want to issue a command but keep the pane open, split the pane and then issue the command with send-keys as you did in Scripting a Project Configuration, on page 42. Be sure to add C-m to the send-keys sequence if you want the command to execute.

Opening a Pane in the Current Directory

When you open a new pane, tmux places you in the directory where you originally launched tmux. Sometimes, that's exactly what you want, but if you navigated into another directory in your window or pane, you might want to create a new pane that starts in that directory instead.

You can use the pane_current_path variable tmux provides when you create a new pane. Open Command mode and execute this:

```
split-window -v -c  "#{pane_current_path}"
```

This splits the window horizontally but opens the new terminal session in the same working directory as the current pane or window.

You can add this to your configuration file, too. Instead of changing the existing bindings for splits, add new ones so you can choose the behavior you'd like:

```
workflows/tmux.conf
# Split pane and retain the current directory of existing pane
bind _ split-window -v -c  "#{pane_current_path}"
bind | split-window -h -c "#{pane_current_path}"
```

This configures things so that `Prefix` `_` splits the window horizontally and `Prefix` `|` splits the window vertically.

Issuing Commands in Many Panes Simultaneously

Every once in a while, you might need to execute the same command in multiple panes. You might need to run the same update script on two servers, for example.

Using the set-window-option synchronize-panes on command, anything you type in one pane will be immediately broadcast to the other panes in the current session.

Try it out. Create a new tmux session and split the window into two panes:

```
tmux new-session -s sync -d
tmux split-pane -t sync
tmux attach -t sync
```

Press `Prefix` `:` to enter Command mode and enter set-option synchronize-panes on. Then, in one of the panes, enter the ls command. As you type the command, you'll see both panes update.

Once you've issued the command, you can turn it off with set-option synchronize-panes off.

If you find yourself doing this often, add a shortcut to this in your configuration. Add the following line to map `Prefix` `Ctrl`-`s` to trigger synchronization:

workflows/tmux.conf
```
# Shortcut for synchronize-panes toggle
bind C-s set-window-option synchronize-panes
```

By not specifying the off or on option, the synchronize-panes command acts as a toggle. While this isn't something you'll use very often, it's amazingly handy when you need it.

Using a Popup Window

If you need a quick way to run a command but don't want to create a new window or pane, you can use a popup window. This window opens over the top of the existing windows.

Try it out. Run the top command in a popup window. In a tmux session, open Command mode with `Prefix` `:` and type the following command:

```
display-popup -E "top"
```

The -E option ensures the popup closes when the program exits. If you omit this, you have to press the `ESC` key to dismiss the window once the program completes.

When you execute the command, the top program runs in the foreground window, as shown in the image on page 78.

Press `q` to quit top and the window closes.

When you create a popup window, you can specify its on-screen position and dimensions, as well as the starting directory and any environment options you need. Execute the following command to open a new popup window with the directory set to your home directory, the position centered vertically and

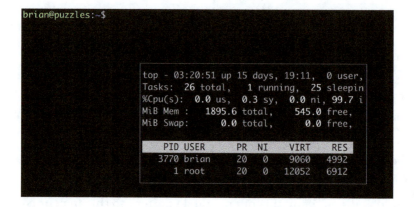

horizontally, the width and height to 50 percent, and an environment variable called POPUP set to true:

```
display-popup -d "~/" \
    -x C -y C -w 50% -h 50% \
    -e "POPUP=true" -E "bash"
```

You can pass multiple environment variables by using additional -e flags.

Of course, you can use a keybinding to trigger this popup. Add this line to bind the popup window to Prefix O :

workflows/tmux.conf
```
bind O display-popup -d "~/" \
                     -x C -y C -w 50% -h 50% \
                     -e "POPUP=true" -E "bash"
```

You've explored a few more ways to work with windows and panes. Next, you'll tame your tmux sessions.

Managing Sessions

As you get more comfortable with tmux, you may find yourself using more than one tmux session simultaneously. For example, you may fire up unique tmux sessions for each application you're working on so you can keep the environments contained. There are some great tmux features to make managing these sessions painless.

Moving Between Sessions

Your tmux sessions all route through a shared tmux server on your machine. That means you can move effortlessly between sessions from a single client. If you have two projects, each in their own tmux session, you can jump between them instead of detaching from one and reattaching to the other.

To try this out, start two detached tmux sessions, one named editor which launches Vim and the other running the top command, called processesk:

```
$ tmux new -s editor -d vim
$ tmux new -s processes -d top
```

Connect to the editor session:

```
$ tmux attach -t editor
```

Then press Prefix (to go to the previous session and Prefix) to move to the next session.

You can customize the keybindings for this to your .tmux.conf file by binding keys to the switch-client command. The default configuration looks like this:

```
bind  ( switch-client -p
bind  ) switch-client -n
```

You can also use Prefix s to display a list of sessions so you can quickly navigate between sessions:

This view shows you all of your sessions and shows a preview of each session when you select it.

Use the j and k keys to move up and down if you've configured tmux to use Vim-like movement. Press Enter to switch to the session. You can press Space to expand a session so you can jump to a specific window or pane within that session. You can also press x to kill a session, which makes this a quick way to close down sessions you no longer need.

tmux sorts the sessions by number in this view, but add the following line to your configuration file to sort the sessions by their names instead:

```
workflows/tmux.conf
# make session chooser order by name instead of session index
bind s choose-tree -sZ -O name
```

Pressing Prefix w opens a similar interface that shows all panes and windows expanded by default, giving you a complete view of all of your sessions and windows.

If you've set up multiple workspaces, this is an extremely efficient way to move around your environments without detaching and reattaching.

Moving Windows Between Sessions

You can move a window from one session to another. This is handy in case you've started up a process in one environment and want to move it around or want to consolidate your workspaces.

The move-window command is mapped to Prefix . (the period), so you can bring up the window you want to move, press the key combination, and then type the name of the target session.

To try this out, create two sessions with the names editor and processes, running vim and top respectively:

```
$ tmux new -s editor -d vim
$ tmux new -s processes -d top
```

Move the window in the processes session into the editor session. First, attach to the processes session:

```
$ tmux attach -t processes
```

Then, press Prefix . and type editor in the command line that appears.

This removes the only window in the processes session, causing it to close. If you attach to the editor session, you'll see both windows.

You can use shell commands to do this, too, so you don't need to attach to sessions to consolidate things. To do that, use tmux move-window in your terminal window like this:

```
$ tmux move-window -s processes:1 -t editor
```

This moves the first window of the processes session to the editor session. Once again, this assumes you set the window and pane base indexes to 1 instead of 0 when you configured tmux in Chapter 2, Configuring tmux, on page 15.

Creating a New Session Without Leaving tmux

You can navigate between tmux sessions, but if you discover you need a brand new tmux session for some work, you don't have to launch a new terminal window.

Enter Command mode with `Prefix` `:` and issue the new-session or new command. You can pass it all of the same options you would pass if you called tmux new-session in a regular terminal window.

For example, inside an existing tmux session, enter Command mode and type the following command to create a new session called "database_project" that opens in the ~/dev/databases directory:

```
new-session -s database_project -c ~/dev/databases
```

Executing this command brings the new session into focus. If you add the -d flag, the new session will start in a detached state, and you could switch to it manually using `Prefix` `s`.

Creating or Attaching to Existing Sessions

Throughout the book, you've taken the approach of creating new tmux sessions whenever you want to try something out. As you make tmux part of your workflow, you may find you want to create a new session if it doesn't already exist or connect to it if it does.

The has-session command returns an exit code that you can use in a shell script, which means you can check to see if the session exists. You saw this back in Scripting a Project Configuration, on page 42 when you detected the session:

```
scripting/reattach/development
if ! tmux has-session -t development
then
  tmux new-session -s development -n editor -d
fi
tmux attach -t development
```

The has-session command is great for scripting complex setups, but tmux has a built-in way of creating a new session or attaching to an existing one—pass the -A flag to the new-session command:

```
$ tmux new-session -A -s development
```

By providing the -A option, tmux will attach to the specified session if it exists or create a new one if it doesn't find it. No need for any shell scripting.

You now have a few more ways to work with your tmux sessions. Next, you'll integrate tmux with your OS.

tmux and Your Operating System

As tmux becomes part of your workflow, you may want to integrate it more tightly with your operating system. In this section, you'll discover ways to make tmux and your system work well together.

Using a Different Shell

tmux will use your default shell when you start a new session or window. You can override the shell tmux uses by explicitly setting the default shell in .tmux.conf. So, if you're on macOS and your default shell is zsh but you'd like to use the Bash shell in tmux, add the following line to your configuration:

```
set -g default-shell /bin/bash
```

Since tmux is just a terminal multiplexer and not a shell of its own, you specify exactly what shell to run when it starts.

Launching tmux by Default

You can configure your system to launch tmux automatically when you open a terminal. Using what you know about session names, you can create a new session if one doesn't exist or attach to one that does.

When tmux is running, it creates a TMUX_PANE environment variable. You can use this value in your shell configuration script to determine whether or not you're currently in a tmux session and conditionally launch tmux if it isn't running already.

For example, you could add these lines to the end of your .bashrc, .bash_profile, or .zshrc file:

```
if [[ -z "$TMUX_PANE" ]]; then
  tmux new-session -A -s "${USER}"
fi
```

This first checks that you are not already in a tmux session by checking whether the TMUX_PANE environment variable is set. If it's empty, this means you're not already in a session. If no session is found, it creates or attaches to a session with a session name of $USER, which is your username. You can replace this with any value you want, but using the username helps avoid conflicts.

When the tmux session starts up, it will run through your .bashrc or .bash_profile file again, but this time it will see that you're in a tmux session, skip over this chunk of code, and execute the rest of the commands in your configuration file, ensuring that all your environment variables are set for you.

Now, every time you open a new terminal, you'll be in a tmux session. Be careful, though, since each time you open a new terminal session on your machine, it will be attached to the same session. Exiting tmux in one terminal will exit tmux in all of them. Be sure to detach from the session first.

Keeping OS-Specific Configuration Separate

In Chapter 4, Working With Text and Buffers, on page 53, you integrated tmux with the macOS and Linux system clipboards, and this involved adding some specific configuration options to your .tmux.conf file. But, if you wanted your configuration to work on both operating systems, you'd run into some conflicts.

The solution is to move your OS-specific configuration into a separate file and then tell tmux to load it up by using tmux's if-shell command and the source command.

Try it out. Create a new file called .tmux.mac.conf in your home directory:

```
$ touch ~/.tmux.mac.conf
```

In that file, put all the code to make the macOS clipboard work with tmux:

```
workflows/tmux.mac.conf
# Prefix Ctrl-C takes what's in the buffer and sends it to system clipboard
# via pbcopy
bind C-c run "tmux save-buffer - | pbcopy"

# y in copy mode takes selection and sends it to system clipboard via pbcopy
bind-key -T copy-mode-vi y send-keys -X copy-pipe-and-cancel "pbcopy"

# Prefix Ctrl-v fills tmux buffer from system clipboard via pbpaste, then
# pastes from buffer into tmux window
bind C-v run "tmux set-buffer \"$(pbpaste)\"; tmux paste-buffer"
```

Then, open .tmux.conf and remove any lines related to macOS if you've put them in. Then add the following code to the end of the file:

```
workflows/tmux.conf
# Load mac-specific settings
if-shell "uname | grep -q Darwin" "source-file ~/.tmux.mac.conf"
```

The if-shell command runs a shell command, and if it's successful, it executes the step. In this case, you tell tmux to run the uname command and use grep to see if it contains the word Darwin. If it does, it's a safe bet you're on a Mac, so it loads the configuration file.

You would use a similar approach to load an additional bit of configuration only if it exists. For example, you may want to share your main .tmux.conf file with the world on GitHub, but you may want to keep some of your own secret sauce private. So, move all of those tricks into .tmux.private, and add this to your .tmux.conf file:

workflows/tmux.conf

```
# Load private settings if they exist
if-shell "[ -f ~/.tmux.private]" "source ~/.tmux.private"
```

This will only load the file if it exists.

Recording Program Output to a Log

Sometimes, it's useful to be able to capture the output of a terminal session to a log. You already used capture-pane and save-buffer to do this, but tmux can actually record the activity in a pane right to a text file with the pipe-pane command. This is similar to the script command available on macOS and Linux, except that with pipe-pane, you can toggle it on and off at will, and you can start it after a program is already running.

To activate this, enter Command mode and type pipe-pane -o "cat >> mylog.txt".

You can use the -o flag to toggle the output, which means if you send the exact command again, you can turn the logging off. Add this to your configuration script to add a key binding that toggles capturing the pane on and off:

workflows/tmux.conf

```
# Log output to a text file on demand
bind P pipe-pane -o "cat >>~/#W.log" \; display "Toggled logging to ~/#W.log"
```

Now, you can press Prefix P to toggle logging. Thanks to the display command (short for display-message), you'll see the name of the log file displayed in the status line. The display and pipe-pane commands have access to the same variables as the status line, which you used in Table 1, Status Line Variables, on page 33.

Adding Battery Life to the Status Line

If you use tmux on a laptop, you may want to show the remaining battery life in your status line, especially if you run your terminal in full-screen mode. Thanks to the #(shell-command) variable, you can integrate the results of a process into your status bar.

Try it out by adding the battery status to your configuration file. Grab a shell script that can fetch the remaining battery charge and display it to the screen. You'll place this in a file called battery in your home folder and tell tmux to run it.

First, download the file:

```
$ curl -L -O \
    https://raw.githubusercontent.com/richo/battery/master/bin/battery
```

You can also find the battery script in the book's source code downloads.

Now, make it executable so tmux can use it:

```
$ chmod +x ~/battery
```

Now, test it out.

```
$ ~/battery
```

If you're running this on a laptop without the power cord plugged in, you'll see the percentage left on the battery.

You can get tmux to display the output of any command-line program in its status bar by using #(<command>). So, to display the battery in front of the clock, change the set -g status-right line in your .tmux.conf to the following:

```
# Status line right side -  31-Oct 13:37
set -g status-right "#[fg=purple]#(~/battery Discharging) | #[fg=cyan]%d %b %R"
```

This displays the battery in purple, separates the battery indicator from the clock with a pipe character, and displays the date and time as before.

When you reload the .tmux.conf file and your laptop is unplugged, the battery status indicator will appear.

```
Session: development 2 1          1:bash- 2:console*          82% | 30 Sep 19:51
```

You can use this approach to customize your status line further. You'd simply need to write your own script that returns the value you want to display and then drop it into the status line.

Integrating Seamlessly with Vim

The Vim text editor works well with tmux, but developer Mislav Marohnić developed a solution that lets you move between tmux panes and Vim splits seamlessly. To make this work, you'll need to install Chris Toomey's vim-tmux-navigator plugin for Vim[1] and add some keybindings to your .tmux.conf file.

---

1.   https://github.com/christoomey/vim-tmux-navigator

This setup will create the following keybindings:

- Ctrl - j moves up

- Ctrl - k moves down

- Ctrl - h moves left

- Ctrl - l moves right

If you're in tmux and you move into Vim, the Vim plugin will take over. If you're in Vim and you move to tmux, tmux will take over. Instead of having to learn two sets of commands to navigate, you just have one.

You can install the plugin using Vundle, Vim-Plug, or other plugin managers, or, if you're using Vim 8 and above, you can use Git to clone the plugin into the ~/.vim/pack/plugin/start/ directory:

```
$ git clone https://github.com/christoomey/vim-tmux-navigator.git\
~/.vim/pack/plugins/start/vim-tmux-navigator
```

Then, in your .tmux.conf file, add these lines to detect Vim and add the keybindings for tmux:

workflows/tmux.conf
```
# Vim and tmux window switching
is_vim="ps -o state= -o comm= -t '#{pane_tty}' \
    | grep -iqE '^[^TXZ ]+ +(\\S+\\/)?g?(view|l?n?vim?x?|fzf)(diff)?$'"
bind -n C-h if-shell "$is_vim" "send-keys C-h"  "select-pane -L"
bind -n C-j if-shell "$is_vim" "send-keys C-j"  "select-pane -D"
bind -n C-k if-shell "$is_vim" "send-keys C-k"  "select-pane -U"
bind -n C-l if-shell "$is_vim" "send-keys C-l"  "select-pane -R"
bind -n 'C-\\' if-shell \"$is_vim\" 'send-keys C-\\\\\'  'select-pane -l'

bind -T copy-mode-vi 'C-h' select-pane -L
bind -T copy-mode-vi 'C-j' select-pane -D
bind -T copy-mode-vi 'C-k' select-pane -U
bind -T copy-mode-vi 'C-l' select-pane -R
bind -T copy-mode-vi 'C-\' select-pane -l

bind C-l send-keys 'C-l'
```

Ctrl - l is the keybinding used by the readline library in many shells for clearing the screen, and the lines you added overrode that keystroke. The last line in this configuration adds one more keybinding that sets up Prefix Ctrl - l to issue the clear command instead.

Customizing Your Workflow

Throughout the book, you've added your own configuration options and changed how tmux looks, but there are additional ways to make tmux work for you. You can hook into tmux's lifecycle events, and you can add community-developed plugins. Start by defining your own popup menu that holds your most-used shortcuts.

Accessing Shortcuts Through a Popup Menu

tmux relies on a lot of keyboard shortcuts. If you memorize those, you can move quickly through a lot of tasks. But sometimes, you might want to have some common commands readily accessible so you can select what you want.

You can build a custom popup menu like this, containing any options you would like:

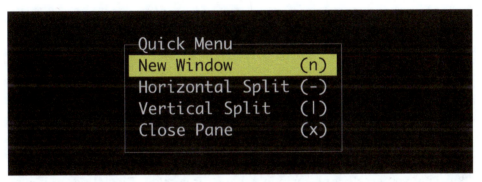

You build this popup menu with the display-menu command. To use this command, you specify the name of the menu item, an associated shortcut key, and the command to execute.

In a tmux session, enter Command Mode (Prefix :) and enter the following command to display a menu with a single option:

```
display-menu "New Window" n "new-window"
```

When you execute the command, the menu appears. You can press ESC to dismiss the menu and Enter or n to select the item.

Like popup windows, you can specify the x and y coordinates, and you can also give the menu a title:

```
display-menu -T "Quick Menu" -x C -y C "New Window" n "new-window"
```

Add additional menu items the same way. Enter the following command all on the same line into Command Mode to display a second option:

```
display-menu -T "Quick Menu" -x C -y C "New Window" n "new-window"
"Horizontal Split" - "split-window"
```

The menu appears with two options. You can navigate the options with the arrow keys or use j and k if you've configured Vim navigation in tmux. You can also select an item with its shortcut.

To define a menu that's bound to a keystroke, pass the menu to the bind-key command. Add the following to your configuration to define a menu that appears when you press Prefix e :

workflows/tmux.conf
```
# popup menu
bind e  \
  display-menu -T "Quick Menu" -x C -y C \
    "New Window" n "new-window" \
    "Horizontal Split" - "split-window" \
    "Vertical Split"  | "split-window -h" \
    "Close Pane" x "kill-pane"
```

You can use any tmux command in a menu, so you could have menu entries that execute external commands, spawn other windows, run your tests, or anything you can think of.

Hooking into tmux Events

tmux hooks let you automate actions in response to specific events within tmux, like when you create a new window, pane, or session. By setting up hooks, you can ensure certain tasks happen automatically. For example, you can apply a certain layout when you split panes, run initialization scripts when a client attaches to a session, or display helpful messages. Hooks let you customize and extend tmux to fit your workflow.

To create a hook, you use the set-hook command, which you can do through Command mode or in the tmux configuration file. You specify the name of the event and the command you want to execute when the event occurs.

Try it out by adding a hook that prints "Welcome to my tmux session" in the status line whenever a client attaches to the current session.

Start a new tmux session called hooks:

```
$ tmux new-session -s hooks
```

Enter Command mode with Prefix : and enter the following command:

```
set-hook client-attached "display-message 'Welcome to my tmux session.'"
```

In another terminal window, attach to the session:

```
$ tmux attach -t hooks
```

The message appears in the new client's status line.

tmux has hooks for events and operations. Most tmux commands have an after- hook that fires immediately after the command. For example, to make tmux resize the panes when you create a new pane, use the after-split-window hook:

```
set-hook after-split-window "select-layout even-vertical"
```

The tmux manual lists many of the available hooks, but the following list shows some of the more useful ones:

Hook	Description
after-new-session	Runs after a new session is created
after-new-window	Runs after a new new is created
after-split-window	Runs after you create a new pane
alert-activity	Runs when a window has activity
client-attached	Runs when a client attaches to a session
session-created	Runs when a session is created
window-resized	Runs when a window is resized

You can use any tmux command in a hook, so there are lots of possibilities. For example, every time you open a new window, have tmux list the directory by using send-keys:

```
set-hook after-new-window "send-keys ls Enter"
```

By default, hooks only apply to the current tmux session. When the session disappears, the hooks go away with it. However, you can remove a hook with set-hook -u:

```
set-hook -u after-new-window
```

If you define the hook again with a different action, the new definition replaces the old one.

You can define a hook to target a specific session using -t, or you can define them globally with -g. To make all new windows list the current directory, define the hook like this:

```
set-hook -g after-new-window "send-keys ls Enter"
```

Note that this is a global hook because it uses the -g option. It applies to all sessions. To remove it, you also need to specify the -g option:

```
set-hook -g -u after-new-window
```

You can use multiple commands in a single hook by separating them with semicolons. Take a look at this hook and see if you can tell what it does:

```
set-hook after-new-window "split-window; split-window -v; select-layout tiled"
```

This sets a hook so that every time you create a new window, tmux splits it into three panes and changes the layout to a tiled layout. In the end, you will have two smaller panes on top of one larger pane on the bottom.

The after- hooks won't fire if their associated command is called by another hook. That means if you have an after-split-window hook defined, calling split-window in another hook won't invoke it.

You can list hooks with the show-hooks command:

```
after-new-window[0] split-window ; split-window -v ; select-layout tiled
```

Using show-hooks without any flags shows you the hooks for your session. Using show-hooks -g shows you a list of global hooks for the session. This isn't the complete list of available hooks you can create, though. Some hooks are global but specific to windows rather than sessions. To see those, run show-hooks -w -g.

tmux stores hooks in an array for each event, which means you can create a series of actions attached to a hook. By default, using set-hook removes all the previous actions for the hook, but if you specify an index, you can add multiple actions without resorting to semicolons. Here's an example that lists the directory contents, splits the window, sets the tiled layout, selects the top pane, and then calls the uname command:

```
set-hook after-new-window[0] "send-keys ls Enter"
set-hook after-new-window[1] "split-window"
set-hook after-new-window[2] "select-layout tiled"
set-hook after-new-window[3] "select-pane -U"
set-hook after-new-window[4] "send-keys uname Enter"
```

Like other tmux commands, you can add set-hook statements to your configuration file so they're always active.

Extending tmux with Plugins

So far, you've made modifications directly to the tmux configuration file. While that works, it can be a little awkward when doing something more complex. Bruno Sutic developed a solution to this called TPM, the tmux plugin manager. Since then, more and more people have come together to build plugins to extend tmux. You can use TPM to install the incredibly useful tmux-resurrect[2] plugin, which can restore tmux sessions even after a reboot.

To set it up, first, clone the repository into a folder called ~/.tmux/plugins/tpm:

```
$ git clone https://github.com/tmux-plugins/tpm ~/.tmux/plugins/tpm
```

Then, add these lines to your .tmux.conf file:

```
workflows/tmux.conf
# tmux plugin manager
set -g @plugin 'tmux-plugins/tpm'
set -g @plugin 'tmux-plugins/tmux-resurrect'
run '~/.tmux/plugins/tpm/tpm'
```

First, you list TPM itself, followed by the tmux-resurrect plugin. Then, you start TPM so it can load other plugins. Save your configuration file and reload your configuration. Then, press `Prefix` `I` to install the plugin. You'll see this output in tmux:

```
Already installed "tpm"

Installing "tmux-resurrect"
  "tmux-resurrect" download success

TMUX environment reloaded.

Done; press ENTER to continue.
```

Now, test out the tmux-resurrect program. Open a couple more panes, and then press `Prefix` `Ctrl`-`s` to save the state of the tmux session. Then, close all of the panes and exit tmux. Finally, reload tmux and press `Prefix` `Ctrl`-`r` to restore the session you saved. All of your panes will come back!

Visit the list of tmux plugins[3] and find one you'd like to install. You'll find one for the battery meter you set up, another for OS-specific clipboard support, and even one with sensible configuration options similar to the ones you've configured in this book. Experiment with each and find a configuration right for you.

What's Next?

There's so much more you can do with tmux now that you know the basics and you've had some experience playing around with various configurations. The tmux manual, which you can access from your terminal with

```
$ man tmux
```

has the complete list of configuration options and available commands.

---

2. https://github.com/tmux-plugins/tmux-resurrect
3. https://github.com/tmux-plugins

And don't forget that tmux itself is rapidly evolving. The next version will bring new configuration options, which will give you even more flexibility.

As you integrate tmux into your workflow, you may discover other techniques you start to rely on. For example, you can use tmux and a text-based editor on a remote server to create an incredibly effective development environment that you can use to collaborate with another developer. You can even use irssi (a terminal-based IRC client) and Alpine (a terminal-based email app) within your tmux sessions, either alongside of your text editor in a pane or in background windows. Then, you can detach from the session and come back to it later with your entire environment ready to go.

Keep working with tmux and before you know it, it'll be an indispensable part of your workflow.

For Future Reference

Command	Description
Prefix !	Converts the currently selected pane into a new window
join-pane -s [session]:[window].[pane]	Converts the specified session's window or pane into a pane in the current window
join-pane -s [session]:[window].[pane] -t [other session]	Converts the specified session's window or pane into a pane in the target session
Prefix z	Zooms the current pane, making it full screen. Pressing it again restores the pane to its original size.
tmux new-session "[command]"	Launches tmux and executes a command. When the command completes, the tmux session closes.
split-pane "[command]"	Splits the current window and executes the specified command in the new pane. When the command completes, the pane closes.
split-window -c "#{pane_current_path}"	Splits the pane and sets the working directory of the new pane to the current working directory of the focused pane
set-option synchronize-panes	Toggles pane synchronization, where keystrokes are issued to all panes simultaneously instead of only the current pane

Command	Description
display-popup [command]	Displays a popup window and runs an optional command. Use -E to make the window close when the command finishes.
Prefix (	Moves to the next tmux session
Prefix)	Moves to the previous tmux session
Prefix s	Shows the session selection list
Prefix w	Shows the session selection list with all windows expanded
move-window -s [source session]: [window] -t [target session]	Moves a window from one session to another. Also available with Prefix ., followed by the target session name
set -g default-shell [shell]	Sets the default shell that tmux uses when creating new windows
set -g default-command [command]	Sets the default command that tmux uses when creating new windows. Blank by default
if-shell "[condition]" "[command]"	Performs a given *command* if the *condition* evaluates to true
pipe-pane -o "cat >>~/#W.log"	Records the current pane to a text file
display-menu -T [menu name] [Entry name] [shortcut] [command]	Displays a popup menu where -T is the title and menu entries are specified with an entry name, shortcut key, and command
set-hook [hook name] "[command to run]"	Creates a hook in the current session
set-hook -g [hook name] "[command to run]"	Creates a hook globally
show-hooks	Show defined hooks for the current session
show-hooks -g	Show defined and available hooks for the global context
show-hooks -g -w	Show defined and available global hooks related to windows

Your Configuration

Throughout the book, you've built up a somewhat complex .tmux.conf file. Here's the entire file for your reference.

workflows/tmux.conf

```
# Set the prefix from C-b to C-a
set -g prefix C-a

# Free the original Ctrl-b prefix keybinding
unbind C-b

# Set the delay between prefix and command
set -s escape-time 1

# Ensure that we can send Ctrl-A to other apps
bind C-a send-prefix

# Set the base index for windows to 1 instead of 0
set -g base-index 1

# Set the base index for panes to 1 instead of 0
set -w -g pane-base-index 1

# Reload the file with Prefix r
bind r \
    source-file ~/.tmux.conf \; \
    display-message "Configuration reloaded"

# Split panes with | and -
bind | split-window -h
bind - split-window -v

# Move between panes with Prefix h,j,k,l
bind h select-pane -L
bind j select-pane -D
bind k select-pane -U
bind l select-pane -R

# Quick window selection
bind -r C-h select-window -t :-
bind -r C-l select-window -t :+
```

```
# Pane resizing panes with Prefix H,J,K,L
bind -r H resize-pane -L 5
bind -r J resize-pane -D 5
bind -r K resize-pane -U 5
bind -r L resize-pane -R 5

# Mouse support - set to on if you want to use the mouse
set -g mouse off

# Set the default terminal mode to 256color mode
set -g default-terminal "tmux-256color"

# Override terminal so it displays 32bit RGB color
set -a terminal-overrides ",*256col*:RGB"

# Set the status line's colors
set -g status-style fg=white,bg=black

# Set the color of the window list
set -g window-status-style fg=cyan,bg=black

# Set colors for the active window
set -g window-status-current-style fg=white,bold,bg=red

# Colors for pane borders
set -w -g pane-border-style fg=green,bg=black
set -w -g pane-active-border-style fg=black,bg=yellow

# Oane border style: single, double, heavy, simple, number.
set -w -g pane-border-lines single

# Add indicators for two-pane setup
set -g pane-border-indicators arrows

# Add status to panes
set -g pane-border-status top

# Active pane normal, other shaded out
set -g window-style fg=color240,bg=color235
set -g window-active-style fg=white,bg=black

# Command / message line
set -g message-style fg=white,bg=color242,bold

# Status line left side to show Session: [name] [window] [pane]
set -g status-left-length 40
set -g status-left "#[fg=green]Session: #S #[fg=yellow]#I #[fg=cyan]#P"

# Status line right side -  31-Oct 13:37
set -g status-right "#[fg=purple]#(~/battery Discharging) | #[fg=cyan]%d %b %R"

# Update the status line every sixty seconds
set -g status-interval 60

# Center the window list in the status line
set -g status-justify centre
```

```
# Enable activity alerts
set -w -g monitor-activity on
set -w -g visual-activity on

# Enable vi keys.
set -w -g mode-keys vi

# Escape turns on copy mode
bind Escape copy-mode-vi

# v in copy mode starts making selection
bind -T copy-mode-vi v send -X begin-selection

# Make Prefix p paste the buffer.
unbind p
bind p paste-buffer

# Shortcut for synchronize-panes toggle
bind C-s set-window-option synchronize-panes

# Split pane and retain the current directory of existing pane
bind _ split-window -v -c  "#{pane_current_path}"
bind \ split-window -h -c  "#{pane_current_path}"

# make session chooser order by name instead of session index
bind s choose-tree -sZ -O name

# Log output to a text file on demand
bind P pipe-pane -o "cat >>~/#W.log" \; display "Toggled logging to ~/#W.log"

# Load mac-specific settings
if-shell "uname | grep -q Darwin" "source-file ~/.tmux.mac.conf"

# Load private settings if they exist
if-shell "[ -f ~/.tmux.private]" "source ~/.tmux.private"

# Vim and tmux window switching
is_vim="ps -o state= -o comm= -t '#{pane_tty}' \
    | grep -iqE '^[^TXZ ]+ +(\\S+\\/)?g?(view|l?n?vim?x?|fzf)(diff)?$'"
bind -n C-h if-shell "$is_vim" "send-keys C-h"  "select-pane -L"
bind -n C-j if-shell "$is_vim" "send-keys C-j"  "select-pane -D"
bind -n C-k if-shell "$is_vim" "send-keys C-k"  "select-pane -U"
bind -n C-l if-shell "$is_vim" "send-keys C-l"  "select-pane -R"
bind -n 'C-\\' if-shell \"$is_vim\" 'send-keys C-\\\\'  'select-pane -l'

bind -T copy-mode-vi 'C-h' select-pane -L
bind -T copy-mode-vi 'C-j' select-pane -D
bind -T copy-mode-vi 'C-k' select-pane -U
bind -T copy-mode-vi 'C-l' select-pane -R
bind -T copy-mode-vi 'C-\' select-pane -l

bind C-l send-keys 'C-l'


bind O display-popup -d "~/" \
                     -x C -y C -w 50% -h 50% \
                     -e "POPUP=true" -E "bash"
```

```
# popup menu
bind e  \
  display-menu -T "Quick Menu" -x C -y C \
    "New Window" n "new-window" \
    "Horizontal Split" - "split-window" \
    "Vertical Split"  | "split-window -h" \
    "Close Pane" x "kill-pane"

# tmux plugin manager
set -g @plugin 'tmux-plugins/tpm'
set -g @plugin 'tmux-plugins/tmux-resurrect'
run '~/.tmux/plugins/tpm/tpm'
```

Thank you!

We hope you enjoyed this book and that you're already thinking about what you want to learn next. To help make that decision easier, we're offering you this gift.

Head on over to https://pragprog.com right now, and use the coupon code BUYANOTHER2025 to save 30% on your next ebook. Offer is void where prohibited or restricted. This offer does not apply to any edition of *The Pragmatic Programmer* ebook.

And if you'd like to share your own expertise with the world, why not propose a writing idea to us? After all, many of our best authors started off as our readers, just like you. With up to a 50% royalty, world-class editorial services, and a name you trust, there's nothing to lose. Visit https://pragprog.com/become-an-author/ today to learn more and to get started.

Thank you for your continued support. We hope to hear from you again soon!

The Pragmatic Bookshelf

SAVE 30%!
Use coupon code
BUYANOTHER2025

Exercises for Programmers

When you write software, you need to be at the top of your game. Great programmers practice to keep their skills sharp. Get sharp and stay sharp with more than fifty practice exercises rooted in real-world scenarios. If you're a new programmer, these challenges will help you learn what you need to break into the field, and if you're a seasoned pro, you can use these exercises to learn that hot new language for your next gig.

Brian P. Hogan
(118 pages) ISBN: 9781680501223. $24
https://pragprog.com/book/bhwb

Serverless Single Page Apps

Don't waste your time building an application server. See how to build low-cost, low-maintenance, highly available, serverless single page web applications that scale into the millions of users at the click of a button. Quickly build reliable, well-tested single page apps that stay up and running 24/7 using Amazon Web Services. Avoid messing around with middle-tier infrastructure and get right to the web app your customers want.

Ben Rady
(212 pages) ISBN: 9781680501490. $24
https://pragprog.com/book/brapps

Effective Remote Work

The office isn't as essential as it used to be. Flexible working hours and distributed teams are replacing decades of on-site, open-plan office culture. Wherever you work from nowadays, your colleagues are likely to be somewhere else. No more whiteboards. No more water coolers. And certainly no Ping-Pong. So how can you organize yourself, ship software, communicate, and be impactful as part of a globally distributed workforce? We'll show you how. It's time to adopt a brand-new mindset. Remote working is here to stay. Come and join us.

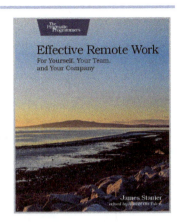

James Stanier
(348 pages) ISBN: 9781680509229. $47.95
https://pragprog.com/book/jsrw

Pomodoro Technique Illustrated

Do you ever look at the clock and wonder where the day went? You spent all this time at work and didn't come close to getting everything done. Tomorrow, try something new. Use the Pomodoro Technique, originally developed by Francesco Cirillo, to work in focused sprints throughout the day. In *Pomodoro Technique Illustrated*, Staffan Nöteberg shows you how to organize your work to accomplish more in less time. There's no need for expensive software or fancy planners. You can get started with nothing more than a piece of paper, a pencil, and a kitchen timer.

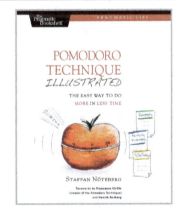

Staffan Nöteberg
(156 pages) ISBN: 9781934356500. $24.95
https://pragprog.com/book/snfocus

New Programmer's Survival Manual

It's your first day on the new job. You've got the programming chops, you're up on the latest tech, you're sitting at your workstation... now what? *New Programmer's Survival Manual* gives your career the jolt it needs to get going: essential industry skills to help you apply your raw programming talent and make a name for yourself. It's a no-holds-barred look at what *really* goes on in the office—and how to not only survive, but thrive in your first job and beyond.

Josh Carter
(256 pages) ISBN: 9781934356814. $29
https://pragprog.com/book/jcdeg

Become a Great Engineering Leader

As you step into senior engineering leadership roles, you need to make an impact, and you need to make it fast. This book will uncover the secrets of what it means to be a successful director of engineering, VP of engineering, or CTO. With a hands-on, practical approach, it will help you understand and develop the skills that you need, ranging from how to manage other managers, to how to define and execute strategy, how to manage yourself and your limited time, and how to navigate your own career journey to your desired destination.

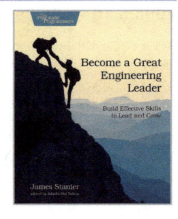

James Stanier
(400 pages) ISBN: 9798888650660. $64.95
https://pragprog.com/book/jsenglb

The Stress Equation

Workplace stress is not the weakness of individuals; it's caused by systemic problems. Armed with the insights in this book, you can identify, analyze, and systematically reduce the factors that lead to poor health, low productivity, and personal burnout. This book gives you a framework for understanding stress, and a vocabulary to make it easier to discuss it among colleagues. Stress can be fixed; find out how.

Marcus Lagré
(126 pages) ISBN: 9798888651018. $35.95
https://pragprog.com/book/stresseq

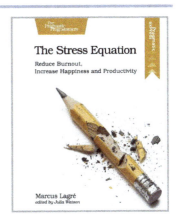

Help Your Boss Help You

Develop more productive habits in dealing with your manager. As a professional in the business world, you care about doing your job the right way. The quality of your work matters to you, both as a professional and as a person. The company you work for cares about making money and your boss is evaluated on that basis. Sometimes those goals overlap, but the different priorities mean conflict is inevitable. Take concrete steps to build a relationship with your manager that helps both sides succeed.

Ken Kousen
(160 pages) ISBN: 9781680508222. $26.95
https://pragprog.com/book/kkmanage

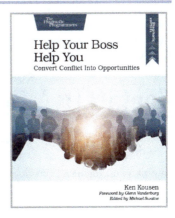

The Pragmatic Bookshelf

The Pragmatic Bookshelf features books written by professional developers for professional developers. The titles continue the well-known Pragmatic Programmer style and continue to garner awards and rave reviews. As development gets more and more difficult, the Pragmatic Programmers will be there with more titles and products to help you stay on top of your game.

Visit Us Online

This Book's Home Page
https://pragprog.com/book/bhtmux3
Source code from this book, errata, and other resources. Come give us feedback, too!

Keep Up-to-Date
https://pragprog.com
Join our announcement mailing list (low volume) or follow us on Twitter @pragprog for new titles, sales, coupons, hot tips, and more.

New and Noteworthy
https://pragprog.com/news
Check out the latest Pragmatic developments, new titles, and other offerings.

Contact Us

Online Orders:	*https://pragprog.com/catalog*
Customer Service:	*support@pragprog.com*
International Rights:	*translations@pragprog.com*
Academic Use:	*academic@pragprog.com*
Write for Us:	*http://write-for-us.pragprog.com*

www.ingramcontent.com/pod-product-compliance
Lightning Source LLC
LaVergne TN
LVHW081346050326
832903LV00024B/1351